How Local Area Networks Work

What They Are and What They Do

BY DAVID R. KOSIUR, PH.D.

JONATHAN ANGEL

Prentice Hall PTR
Englewood Cliffs, New Jersey 07632

Library of Congress Cataloging-in-Publication Data

Kosiur, David R.

How local area networks work : what they are, what they do, c1995
/ by David R. Kosiur, Jonathan Angel.
    p.   cm.
Includes index.
ISBN 0-13-185489-5
1. Local area networks (Computer networks)   I. Title.
TK5105.7.K667   1995
004.6'8'02468--dc20

94-34838
CIP

Prentice-Hall, Inc.
A Simon and Schuster Company
Englewood Cliffs, NJ 07632

Vanstar Corporation, 5964 West Las Positas Blvd., Pleasanton, CA 94588.

The author and publisher have used their best efforts in preparing this book. However, the author and publisher make no warranties of any kind, express or implied, with regard to the information contained herein, and specifically disclaim, without limitation, any implied warranties of merchantability and fitness for a particular purpose with respect to any product herein referred to and/or the techniques described in the book. In no event shall the author or publisher be responsible or liable for any loss of profit or any other commercial damages, including but not limited to special, incidental, consequential or any other damages in connection with or arising out of furnishing, performance or use of this book.

Trademarks

A number of entered words in which we have reason to believe trademark, service mark, or other proprietary rights may exist have been designated as such by initial capitalization. However, no attempt has been made to designate as trademarks or service marks all personal computer words or terms in which proprietary rights might exist. The inclusion, exclusion or definition of a word or term is not intended to affect, or to express any judgment on, the validity or legal status of any proprietary right that may be claimed in that word or term.

Names

Company and personal names used in examples and illustrations are used with permission or are fictional. Any resemblance to real persons or companies from which permission has not been obtained is coincidental.

Prices

All prices included in this book are manufacturers' list price, accurate at press time.

Credits

Interior Design: Marianne Ackerman, Amaryllis Design
Illustrator: Laurie Wigham
Cover Design: Lundgren Graphics
Editor: David Gancher and Alan Rin
Typesetter: Nancy Adams

The publisher offers discounts on this book when ordered in bulk quantities.
For more information, contact: Corporate Sales Department, Prentice Hall PTR, 113 Sylvan Avenue, Englewood Cliffs, NJ 07632,
Phone: 800-382-3419, FAX: 201-592-2249, E-mail: dan_rush@prenhall.com

Printed in the United States of America

10 9 8 7 6 5 4 3 2 1

ISBN 0-13-185489-5

Prentice-Hall International (UK) Limited, London
Prentice-Hall of Australia Pty. Limited, Sydney
Prentice-Hall of Canada, Inc., Toronto
Prentice-Hall Hispanoamericana S.A., Mexico
Prentice-Hall of India Private Limited, New Delhi
Prentice-Hall of Japan, Inc., Tokyo
Simon & Schuster Asia Pte. Ltd., Singapore
Editora Prentice-Hall do Brasil, Ltda., Rio de Janeiro

Contents

4 / Cabling and Connections

5 / LAN Applications

PART TWO

6 / Internetworking

7 / LAN Administration

8 / LAN Security

9 / The Networked Workplace

10 / Buyer's Guide

PART THREE

Bibliography

Glossary

Index

Preface

How Local Area Networks Work is a practical and understandable book on LANs—or local area networks—designed specifically for the business person using computers. A new kind of computer book, it combines elements of technology books and business books to address the distinct needs of the computerized work place, where there may be 5 or 50 thousand employees.

How Local Area Networks Work focuses on the strategic advantages and implications of using LANs. So whether you're a CEO who wants to know how your company's information is shared, a manager who needs to link up the computers in your department, or a smart employee who knows there's a big future in LANs, you'll find this book to be essential reading.

In simple, non-technical language, *How Local Area Networks Work* explains what LANs are and how they are used in business. At the same time, it provides the information your company needs to make network technology work best for you.

This book was produced by Vanstar Corporation, which, in early 1994, changed its name from ComputerLand Corporation. It reflects 17 years of frontline experiences of thousands of Vanstar experts—from systems engineers to corporate trainers, from sales reps to help desk staffers. These people work with all kinds of computer users—employees in small firms as well as in large corporations.

We invite you to benefit from our collective experiences by reading *How Local Area Networks Work*.

—Karen Sharpe,
Publisher

Acknowledgments

We would like to thank the staff of *LAN Magazine* for their assistance in compiling information for this book and for their generosity in providing access to the valuable material they've published over the years.

We especially thank Steve Schneiderman, Editor-in-Chief of *LAN Magazine*, and urge all readers of this book to read his magazine regularly for continuing, up-to-date information and guidance in the rapidly changing world of local area networks.

Our deep thanks, too, to Glenn Massaro, Director of Operations, Networking Services at Vanstar Corporation (formerly called ComputerLand Corporation), and to Steve Steinke, author of *Guide to Managing PC Networks*, who both carefully read the manuscript and offered many useful suggestions. And our grateful appreciation to Jonathan Angel, Vanstar's Products Editor, who not only thoroughly reviewed the book, but also wrote the Buyer's Guide, which appears at the end of the book.

Introduction

A local area network (LAN) takes single "personal" computers and, by linking them to other systems and people, turns them into a "team" computer. When properly installed and operated, a LAN can boost productivity, cut expenses and allow an organization to approach its work in innovative ways.

But unlike standalone PCs, you can't just plug in a LAN and begin using it. Potential owners must first understand the different types of LANs and LAN components, how they work, and how they can be applied to specific situations before they can gain the full benefit of a LAN. That's what this book is for.

The need for LAN technology arose on the day the second PC was built. Shortly after PCs began arriving in offices in the early 1980s, business owners and managers quickly realized that PC users needed a way to exchange information quickly and easily. In the early days of PCs, most users moved files via the low-tech "sneaker net"—running from PC to PC with a floppy disk in hand. PC vendors quickly recognized the opportunity and began marketing, installing and servicing products that could link PCs together by wire. The term "local area network" came into use, signifying a data communications network that spanned a limited geographic area such as an office, a building or a group of buildings.

Over the years, LANs matured from simple file-swapping products into systems that allowed users to share peripherals, exchange electronic mail, work on files collaboratively and access centrally stored information. In short order, many LANs began offering users access to larger mainframe or minicomputers and providing gateways to other networks across the country and around the world.

Today, LANs come in all shapes and sizes, from "lite LANs" that connect a handful of users, to sophisticated networks that routinely handle the demands of thousands of users. No two LANs are alike—each is configured to meet the specific needs of its owner. Your LAN can be tailored to yours.

Since you're reading *How Local Area Networks Work*, we assume that you have an interest in LANs. We also assume that you have some working knowledge of PCs and PC peripherals, but you don't know very much about LANs or how they work. Consequently, this book is aimed at three types of readers:

- Executives, managers and computer users whose companies already have LANs and want to understand how the systems work or how to best use them
- Those whose businesses may be planning to install LANs and need to know more about what they are, how much they cost, how they affect the way businesses operate and how to buy LAN components
- Those whose businesses now use mainframes or minicomputers but are contemplating "downsizing" to LANs.

For all of these readers, *How Local Area Networks Work* has the information they need to understand the capabilities of this new technology and to make an intelligent decision about the appropriate type of LAN to install. We've tried to skip the buzzwords and arcane descriptions that are the hallmark of too many LAN books. In these pages are concise and accurate explanations of the topics, terms and acronyms that may faze some newcomers to the field. You will discover that while LANs are exceedingly complex and powerful systems, the ability to implement a LAN lies within the grasp of any business owner, department manager or smart employee.

This book will help you learn about the hardware, the software and the operating systems that make up a LAN. You'll also become acquainted with the specific applications and uses for LANs in business as well as everyday LAN operation and administration. In addition, Chapter 10, a detailed buyer's guide, will help you learn about and choose between the many LAN products that are now available. It focuses on product categories and types, and avoids specific versions so it won't become outdated. Because of the volatility of the marketplace, we can guarantee the accuracy of the information in the Buyer's Guide only at the time of publication. For the most current information, call the manufacturers, whose numbers are also listed.

We hope this book will provide you with the information you need to understand how a LAN can work for you, helping you to do your business better.

PART ONE

1 / What a LAN Is

A LAN is a data communications network spanning a limited geographical area, a few miles across at most, but more commonly a single office, floor or building. It allows users to communicate by electronic mail and to share information and such computer resources as mass storage, backup facilities, software, printers or pen plotters for blueprints.

Typically, a LAN is made up of hardware, software and connections. The connections and the software are the distinctive part: network interface cards (circuit boards) that fit inside the connected computers; cable to link these computers together; driver and protocol software to move data between computers; user interface software to connect users to network services; and operating system software to actually process the applications' requirements for items such as files and printers.

Through a LAN, an individual personal computer can link up with other personal computers in a workgroup or department. Other network tools can broaden the possible interconnections between computers; they can even connect personal computers with midrange computers and mainframes. Wide area networks, or WANs, can connect personal computers located in different buildings or cities. Often, the LAN is linked to larger LANs or WANs that form a company-wide information system.

LANs generally are brought into two types of offices: those with many separate personal computers and those with mainframes. We will discuss both situations in this chapter, going into the distinctive ways that LANs affect each one.

LANs and the Single-PC Workplace

In many ways, local area networks enable the company equipped with isolated PCs to work with the computing resources of a mainframe. In other ways, the LAN makes possible entirely new forms of business computing that do no less than revolutionize the workplace. Since managers looking to upgrade their offices traditionally were drawn to mainframe technology, let's first discuss the ways that LANs work like "big iron."

Bringing Mainframe Features to the Desktop

When a LAN links together a group of previously unconnected PCs, it brings powers to their users that were once available only on mainframes. One of the major advantages of this type is communications, or sharing of information. With a network service such as electronic mail, for instance, coworkers can easily exchange phone messages, notes about business meetings or plans for the production cycle.

Without a LAN, tasks that involve several steps or related operations can be unmanageably cumbersome. Either they must be done sequentially on a single computer, one step after another, or else information must be transferred among computers via floppy diskettes. For example, a newsletter editor who needs to track successive revisions of articles can attempt to enforce strict diskette labeling and file-naming conventions on all authors and editors. Under the pressure of deadlines, however, something inevitably falls through the cracks. The result is that some corrections are omitted from the final draft or stylistic inconsistencies are not eliminated.

On a LAN, that newsletter or parts of it can be passed quickly over the network for review, or it can be shared as a single editable document among all the people responsible for creating the final draft. A systematic tracking mechanism would be painless and simple on a LAN, saving time and providing common access to such resources as customized spelling dictionaries and style sheets.

A network gives multiple computer users concurrent access to all kinds of data.

This goes beyond just documents; a network gives multiple computer users concurrent access to all kinds of data. Using a multiuser database on a network would, for example, allow a group of employees to fill customer orders, place orders with suppliers, prepare invoices and adjust inventory—all at the same time.

Here are the major mainframe-type benefits of LANs:

- **Communication.** Once a LAN connects the people in your company, every possible form of discourse is possible, from electronic notes to spreadsheets to graphics files and video. People like to communicate, and they can do that on the network quickly and easily, whether the other user is at the next desk or—through a gateway—in another state. Most network users say the benefits of electronic mail alone justify the investment. E-mail is discussed in Chapter 5, LAN Applications.

- **Shared Hardware.** A network gives each user access to any peripheral, from modems and printers to such expensive devices as high-resolution film printers or pen plotters. Using this equipment at maximum efficiency can save your company a great deal.

■ **Shared Information.** The concept is simple: Networks connect each personal computer so that everyone can use the same tools and share the same data—and update common data simultaneously. Networks are especially useful when many users are constantly updating the same files. Data produced jointly within a department can be shared with other parts of the company—or even the public—in a secure database. The servers that make this possible are discussed in Chapter 3, Hardware.

■ **Security.** Even though a network connects many users together and can make access to data more open, it also offers security safeguards for protecting users and their data. Passwords and access codes ensure that only authorized people can read or write to sensitive files. And networks offer another type of security. While single-user systems can lose valuable data when a hard disk malfunctions, network software can protect against data loss by using more than one hard disk drive on the network for data storage. Since duplicate records are being kept, data integrity is virtually assured. Chapter 8, LAN Security, covers this subject.

■ **Productivity.** With a local area network to share computer resources and information, people can do their jobs more quickly, more efficiently and with less hassle. The LAN will quickly become the heart of your business. Chapter 9, The Networked Workplace, goes into this.

New Ways of Working

Beyond the computing benefits that are already familiar to mainframe users, two basic attributes of LANs—their connectivity and their versatility—make possible entirely new ways of using computers to conduct business more efficiently and more effectively.

Connectivity

Networks can be linked in a variety of ways to each other and to much larger systems, including midrange computers and mainframes. Through sophisticated gateways, networks can provide users with ready access to vast information resources—without having to switch from the familiar software that PC users are accustomed to.

Networks can provide users with ready access to vast information resources.

A LAN can help your staff disseminate information to people outside the organization or gather information from them—customer ordering information or account status, vendor parts lists and availability information—via modem using ordinary phone lines. This capability is discussed in Chapter 6, Internetworking.

Flexibility

Networks can start out small and be expanded to meet greater and greater demands. Individual LANs typically serve 5 to 100 users, but by linking together LANs to form larger internetworks, there is virtually no limit to the number of users that can communicate with each other. A LAN can be used to link just a few users, while a complex internetwork can connect an entire company with tens of thousands of employees in many locations. Chapter 6, Internetworking, shows how this is done.

The New World of Groupware

New "groupware" software applications available to LAN users are changing the way entire businesses work. Groupware represents just one of the ways software developers are taking advantage of LAN technology to make their products more useful and powerful. Groupware programs allow teams of users to collaborate on a spreadsheet, report, business presentation or other type of document. Users can make additions, revisions or add notes that other team members can see almost instantly.

In addition, groupware-oriented calendars and appointment schedulers that instantly check schedules of other workers for date and time conflicts make scheduling in-person meetings a snap. This product category is discussed in Chapter 5, LAN Applications.

Software Economies

In most cases, software designed for networks costs less per user than buying individual copies. More importantly, everyone connected by the network can use off-the-shelf software, reducing problems of compatibility while upgrading and making training easier. Also, network users can get the benefits of multiuser systems without having to change software. So there's no need to lose your company's investment in software based on DOS, Windows, Macintosh or OS/2. LAN software is treated in more detail in Chapter 5, LAN Applications.

How LANs Work in Real Life

Different people have different concerns about what a LAN can do for them, depending on the specific job they need to do. Here are some examples from the broad variety of potential LAN users:

A telemarketing department head can have online access to customer account and inventory information stored in a multiuser database. Since entries in the database are updated instantaneously, the phone sales staff won't promise items that are out of stock, and customers won't exceed their credit limits by placing multiple orders before they are posted.

The project leader of a regularly revised training manual, by storing the draft manual on a file server, can make orderly revisions and ensure that each team member works only on the most current version. Workflow software allows the project leader to ensure that each team member receives the document in the right order, for either rewriting or approval.

A regional sales manager can use electronic mail to communicate with salespeople who are always on the phone or on the road, and to collect information needed to prepare reports.

Software designed for networks costs less per user than buying individual copies.

A lead programmer can give each team member access to common library modules stored on a file server and control the proliferation of multiple versions.

A publisher can standardize style specifications, spelling and hyphenation dictionaries to ensure consistency in the company's publications. A publication can go from the writer to the printer with new systems of electronic text management.

An executive assistant can maintain the boss's schedule of meetings or coordinate meetings with other members of the staff by using groupware.

A customer service manager can keep track of returned items as well as the types of problems reported for each product by monitoring a shared database.

LANs and the Mainframe Office

"Downsizing" in the computer world signifies getting rid of old hardware and software in favor of more efficient technologies. Many owners of mainframes are replacing them with more cost-effective distributed LAN systems, which can be far less expensive to configure, operate and maintain. As of this writing, a basic, no-frills LAN server (the computer at the heart of most LANs) can be acquired for less than $3,000, and user workstations, with independent processing and storage capabilities, cost less than $1,000 apiece. Compare these figures with the price of a $100,000 mainframe and "dumb" terminals that sell for about the same price as PC workstations. Furthermore, maintenance and service costs for LAN hardware are usually a fraction of similar mainframe expenses. Employees with less technical skill, moreover, can do a lot of maintenance and troubleshooting.

LANs are designed with ordinary office workers in mind.

Beyond cost, however, LANs offer great operational advantages over mainframes that mean new effectiveness in business and human terms. Some are discussed here; others are detailed in Chapter 9, The Networked Workplace.

Mainframe-based multiuser systems haven't been completely supplanted by PCs and LANs, of course, and perhaps never will be. For example, if a company or office routinely deals with large files of 100 megabytes or more, a big computer is still the way to go. But even airlines and insurance companies—two firms that must deal with vast volumes of data—are recognizing the advantages of linking their mainframes and minicomputers to LANs for routine work. A LAN lets users access minicomputers or mainframes not by making direct connections but by distributing mainframe sessions through a device called a gateway, thus reducing the need to buy terminals in addition to the terminal-emulating PC workstation.

Other LAN software lets users work within their normal PC interface to access and analyze data residing on a mainframe. Chapter 2, Network Operating Systems, covers the basics behind this capability. The issue of connecting LANs to mainframes, minis and even larger LANs is also taken up in Chapter 6, Internetworking.

For the average company or office, a LAN offers the most flexible way of storing information and allowing groups of users to reliably input, access, manipulate and store data. Whereas mainframes and minicomputers were built for computer specialists to use, LANs are designed with ordinary office workers in mind. Ways have been devised to make the big multiuser systems more human-oriented. But such technological afterthoughts don't change the fundamental structure of the systems, which discourage casual communication between users and the local processing of favorite applications and other PC features that LAN users take for granted.

The Software Edge

Compared to big computers, PC-based LANs offer a wealth of software at affordable prices. Many popular program titles are simply not available for mainframe systems, or when they are available, it's usually at a substantially higher price.

LANs also offer an advantage to a company or office that uses custom-designed software. With mainframe and minicomputers on the decline, today's sharpest software developers concentrate on PC-oriented languages and operating systems. Generally speaking, it's easier to find and hire a qualified PC programmer at the right price than a mainframe counterpart. And with many PC applications offering their own scripting and programming languages, companies can take advantage of programs written by their own rank-and-file employees as well as by workers of other companies who distribute their products on the open market.

Chapter 10, Buyer's Guide, shows just some of the wealth of LAN software available.

Training

The costs of user training may be overlooked when deciding whether to downsize from a mainframe environment. Owners of mainframe-based systems must budget vast sums on training just to get people to learn how to operate their machines. LAN owners are much more fortunate. Now that most office professionals know the basics of running a PC as well as the applications that pertain to their work, training costs can be dramatically reduced.

Even when training is necessary, the costs are usually much lower, since PC workers are much further along on the learning curve than mainframe users who must work with proprietary mainframe products. Of course, novice users will need some training both about their personal computer and the network. Training is discussed further in Chapter 9, The Networked Workplace, and Chapter 7, LAN Administration.

"Comprehensive documentation is beneficial as you train and cross-train your staff to handle various situations."
— DAVE MOLTA, SYRACUSE UNIVERSITY

The Advantage of Scalability

Unlike a mainframe-based multiuser system, a LAN can grow in step with the business. Many multiuser environments place a strict limit on the number of users that can be supported—16, 32, 64, 128, 256, or whatever. Exceeding this limit leads to sluggish performance. The only satisfactory way to get around this problem is to upgrade the mainframe, an expensive solution. Mainframe-based multiuser systems require exotic equipment, such as communications and cluster controllers that can drive up the cost of expansion in a hurry.

A LAN, on the other hand, can usually be easily expanded by plugging in new components—a new workstation, server, printer, modem or whatever is called for. LANs can even be linked to other LANs. In fact, most LAN owners find low-tech factors, such as the cost of cabling and dealing with the physical limitations of their office, to be the greatest barriers to network expansion. These matters are dealt with in more detail in Chapter 9, The Networked Workplace.

2 / Network Operating Systems

How Operating Systems Work
Network Architecture
The Client-Server Model
Major Network Operating Systems
The Seven OSI Levels

Now that we understand the basic components of a local area network and how they're connected, let's take a look at what makes a LAN run: the special software that makes it possible for everyone in the system to communicate, share peripherals and resources, transfer files and perform network activity.

There are usually two main parts to network operating system software: workstation software and server software. The workstation software allows each PC to access the services on the network. It reroutes data over the network when needed. The server software makes disks, software and ports available to the PCs on the network.

LAN system software is the controlling brain of the operation. Among the many crucial functions that the system software performs are the following:

- Controlling the operation of the network—who uses it when, what they have access to, which network resources are available
- Moving data around, redirecting it to whatever workstation, server or other resource in the system you have selected
- Providing other crucial administrative tools that add, change and remove users and equipment from the network
- Supporting file and record locking and providing other security features such as different passwords and privilege levels for each user.

How Network Operating Systems Work

In categorizing all the network operating systems for LANs, it's convenient to break them down into two classes: DOS-based and non-DOS-based. DOS-based NOSes, such as LANtastic, work by redirection and depend on the DOS operating system. They aren't the most advanced NOSes, but it is easiest to explain NOSes in general by describing these first. The non-DOS-based NOSes, such as VINES and NetWare, can operate on server platforms other than DOS or Intel computers and do not require DOS-based redirection in order to work.

Redirection

At the heart of the network operating system is a concept called redirection. You are probably familiar with DOS redirection. For example, the command DIR>FILENAME redirects a directory listing to a file instead of to the screen. The ">" tells DOS to give the results of the command on the left to the entity on the right. Thus, the command DIR>LPT1: sends the contents of the directory to your printer instead of to the screen.

The important thing about redirection is that the program, in this case DIR, does not know or care where its output is going. It just sends it to DOS, which then takes care of it, depending on the redirection commands entered by the user.

Network operating systems depend heavily on redirection, only the data is redirected over the network, in pieces called packets, instead of to files or printers.

Network operating systems depend heavily on redirection, only the data is redirected over the network, in pieces called packets, instead of to files or printers. Nevertheless, the operation is almost identical.

Here's how it works. Take, for example, the command COPY C:FILEA F:. This copies FILEA from drive C: to drive F:. For this to work, you must have a drive F:. You could have a drive F: if you had extra hard disks on your PC, or RAM disks, but suppose you don't. Instead you have a drive F: on *another* PC across the building attached via a LAN.

How does this work? The network operating system makes it appear to the COPY program that drive F: is local. The COPY program doesn't know or care that drive F: is across the network. It sends the file to DOS just as it always does, only this time the network operating system steps in to reroute the file over the network to drive F: across the building. Drive F: is an example of a *logical drive* or *virtual drive*.

The same redirection can be done with printers and other peripheral devices. Thus, LPT1: can actually be a printer on the network instead of a local printer and COM1 can be a network modem. The network operating system takes care of redirecting all of these devices. Of course, the user doesn't need to know about redirection, but just types the drive destination or prints from the word processor as usual. The network takes care of the rest.

The Server

When you redirected the output to logical drive F:, the PC at the other end, where drive F: resides, must be expecting data if the COPY command is going to work. It also must have made its hard drive available to users on the network. Again, it is the network operating system that takes care of this, using a component called the server. The server does just what it sounds like—it serves up a computer's resources to the network, making them available for use by other PCs attached to the LAN.

With some network operating systems, the machine with the server part cannot be used as a workstation and is called a dedicated server machine.

Thus, we have a network operating system made up of two parts: a redirector and a server. Not all machines need run a server. But all machines must run some kind of redirector, because every machine has to be able to put data onto the network, and the redirector is the piece that does this.

With some network operating systems, the machine with the server part cannot be used as a workstation and is called a dedicated server machine. Novell uses this kind of setup almost exclusively. With other network operating systems, all machines on the network can be servers if desired. This is a nondedicated server setup and is the basis of peer-to-peer LANs, described later in this chapter.

File Service

The server we have been talking about is a file server. It is called this because its primary task is to make files available to users on the network, even though it might also make other resources available—printers, modems, etc. File service allows users to share files on a PC. The server PC can make its whole disk available, certain directories available, or only certain files available. Often, the network operating system can let the LAN manager determine which users are allowed to use which files, keeping the mail clerk out of the payroll file, for example. In any case, all that is happening with a file server is that its hard disk is becoming an extension of each user's PC. Here's how it works.

Suppose you want to use a file from the file server hard disk. You set up your local drive F: to be the file server hard disk, using the network operating system. The process has many names. Some call it *mapping* the drive to the server disk; others call it *mounting*. In either case you are setting up a virtual drive. Your drive F: is not really local, even though it appears that way to your PC. It is actually the drive on the file server, and the redirection part of the network operating system makes sure that everything destined for drive F: ends up at the file server.

Some call it mapping the drive to the server disk; others call it mounting. In either case you are setting up a virtual drive.

Now suppose the file you want from the hard disk is a word processor, say, *WordPerfect*. From the F: prompt you type the command for *WordPerfect*, WP. What happens next is that *WordPerfect* is loaded into the memory of your PC. The *WordPerfect* file is still sitting on the server while you're running it in your machine. The same is the case for a document file you open from drive F: using *WordPerfect*. It remains on the server while you edit it on your PC.

Meanwhile, other people can use *WordPerfect* from the file server. As for the document you are using, *WordPerfect* must make it clear to other users that you are using it. It does so by locking the file. This prevents others from using it. With some programs, file locking might allow other users to read the document you are editing without making changes to it. They will have to wait until you finish and open the file again. Some network operating systems can provide this kind of file locking for programs that don't. This keeps users from "bumping into" each other.

The important thing to remember about file service is that it is just an extension of the local PC. Programs work just as they would if they were on the local PC. There are some exceptions. Many database programs have been built to take advantage of a file server, allowing many users to work on the same database at the same time. Some, like *Paradox*, even allow one user to see changes made by another. Still, the file server itself is doing nothing more than doling out files. Of course, network operating systems provide much more than just file service—they also provide security, administration, printer sharing, tape backup, fault tolerance and much more.

Server Operation

The file server part of the network operating system makes a PC into a multiuser machine. But we must qualify what we mean by "multiuser." All network operating systems allow many users to share the server PC's peripherals, but not all let them share its processor. DOS-based NOSes are of this second type.

In most cases, the file server has its own non-DOS operating system. NetWare servers do not run DOS—they only emulate it. The same is true of other network operating systems. Novell and Banyan replace DOS with a multitasking operating system, thereby winning performance advantages at the cost of requiring dedicated file servers. Nevertheless, the operation of all file servers is similar and accomplishes the same thing: allowing multiple users to share the peripherals of the file server.

The enhancements that come with non-DOS network operating systems are great. Some new NOSes are based on OS/2, a multitasking PC operating system. That means users with OS/2 can do several things at the same time and OS/2 makes sure these things don't bump into each other. Others use Unix or Windows NT for the same reason.

The biggest advantage of this is that one of the services a server can offer is a task; that is, the server can offer its processor for use by other users, even while it is serving up files and printers. This means a fast server can be used to perform onerous chores like program compiling, calculations and database sorting. It also means new types of programs can be used to take advantage of the server processor.

NetWare servers do not run DOS—they only emulate it.

Instead of just getting files from the server, the server can run programs that work with the programs users are running. The best example of this is a database server. The database server does things like sorting, searching and indexing so the user program and PC don't have to. This cuts down on network traffic, since not so many things are going back and forth between user and server. It also improves performance and security, since the server can handle the database centrally for many users.

This difference—DOS vs. non-DOS network operating systems—is what underlies the two types of LAN architecture, a major division to keep in mind throughout the rest of this book.

Network Architecture

In the computer world, "architecture" stands for the structure of a complete system, including all of the hardware and software components required for proper operation. The simplest type of network architecture is really no network at all, merely a matter of linking two PCs together via their serial ports to exchange files. Packages that allow users to do this include *Brooklyn Bridge* from Fifth Generation Systems (Baton Rouge, La.) and *LapLink* from Traveling Software (Bothell, Wash.).

When it comes to proper networks in which more than two computers are connected together, the two general types of network architecture are called "peer-to-peer" and "client-server." Which type is right for a situation depends on a number of factors, including the size of the network, its cost and the sort of performance needed. Choosing the right architecture for your business is covered further in Chapter 9, The Networked Workplace.

Top-Down Network Design

The best network design philosophy takes a top-down approach, beginning with the people who will use the network. Despite the fact that installation starts at the bottom, with cables and the physical apparatus of the network, you'll get the best results from your network if you start with top-down design concepts.

The Peer-to-Peer Model

Of the two network architectures, peer-to-peer tends to appeal most to small companies and offices that have limited funds to spend on a LAN and personnel with limited technical skills. The technology is also attractive to organizations with significant peripheral sharing demands (printers, modems, etc.) and modest data-sharing needs that can be met by a simple workgroup. For this reason, peer-to-peer LANs are sometimes called "lite" LANs.

Generally speaking, peer-to-peer networks are hindered by memory and performance limitations, compared to client-server LANs. But their relatively low cost makes them an attractive choice for many potential LAN owners.

How It Works

In a peer-to-peer network, a server doesn't have to be an all-powerful, central computer. In fact, any PC on the network can be a server, hence the use of the word "peer." What makes the PC a server in this case is purely software; in client-server LANs, servers are generally different pieces of hardware from PCs.

A peer-to-peer LAN doesn't replace the user's operating system but in fact relies on it. In DOS, one or several simple TSR (terminate-stay-resident) programs handle the networking chores. On the Macintosh, some INITs and a desk accessory are usually all that's needed. Most peer-to-peer LANs come ready to use out of the box. The user merely wires together the PCs, installs the software and the network is ready to run. The different ways of wiring LANs are discussed under the heading "Topologies" in Chapter 4, Cabling and Connections.

Popular peer-to-peer LAN packages for Intel-based computers include Windows for Workgroups from Microsoft Corp., LANtastic from Artisoft, and NetWare Lite from Novell. For Macs, Apple's System 7 includes File Sharing, and LANtastic now offers a version that can be used on Mac networks. The LANtastic system can be used on mixed networks of DOS and Mac computers. DOS users wishing to access Apple's file sharing on Macs running System 7 need Farallon's PhoneNETTalk.

A peer-to-peer network provides a high level of flexibility, since all users can have access to everyone else's files, software, peripherals and other resources. It also can provide a more efficient LAN, since each computer on the network can be a server and store files. That way, if one computer (server) goes down, users can work on data that's stored on another computer. In fact, if somebody should accidentally cut the cable, the cable's ends can be terminated and two separate LANs formed. For even greater flexibility, a centralized server can be added to a peer-to-peer LAN to handle a very large database, video images or other storage-intensive applications.

Administration

Peer-to-peer networks have gained a reputation for being trouble-free, "plug-and-play" products. This reputation is largely deserved as far as users are concerned, but overseeing any network, even one as simple as a peer-to-peer LAN, requires investing time and energy.

Since data is distributed among all the computers acting as servers on the peer-to-peer LAN, location of data may not always be simple. This might also be problematic if a network manager is responsible for backing up all shared data on the LAN. Also, since users are usually responsible for deciding who has access to data stored on their computers, security is usually not as tight as when an administrator controls access rights for a centralized server.

Network security is relatively straightforward on a peer-to-peer LAN. In most cases, the administrator simply issues user IDs to all users and reserves separate and distinct passwords for each account. To enter the LAN, the user merely types in the right ID number and password. To enhance security, the password can be changed by either the user or administrator on a regular basis.

Many peer-to-peer LAN packages also allow the administrator to lock out users from specific files and drives.

Many peer-to-peer LAN packages also allow the administrator to lock out users from specific files and drives. This feature prevents marketing manager John from looking into personnel manager Mary's files. The administrator usually has a special user ID that permits access into all areas of the LAN. Users can also set up user accounts on their own computers to control access to files that are stored on their machine, but shared with others.

Adding users to a peer-to-peer network can be less expensive than with a client-server LAN, particularly for small networks. With most peer-to-peer products, adding users can be done on a one-at-a-time basis, as opposed to server-based expansion, which often requires new licenses in increments of five, ten and so forth.

Some Drawbacks

The previously noted memory and performance limitations make peer-to-peer LANs a poor choice for businesses that need to link together large numbers of PC users. Getting peer-to-peer LANs to work with other networks is difficult, and the limited number of management tool products only compounds the difficulties.

Some peer-to-peer LAN package vendors boast as many as 250 to 300 users per network. But in the real world, most peer-to-peer LANs are considerably smaller—one or two dozen users at most. With more than a couple of dozen workstations, LAN performance decreases noticeably and the length of time required to save or retrieve data becomes unacceptable. The more users added, the slower the performance. At some point, the LAN owner must either spin some users off into another network or look for a technology that can handle more users, specifically a client-server arrangement.

The Client-Server Model

While a peer-to-peer LAN is typically based on DOS and TSR programs, a client-server network uses a powerful network operating system, such as NetWare, OS/2 or Unix. The client-server name identifies the way the LAN operates. In the client-server model, intelligent "client" PCs (not terminals) request services from a server—a high-end PC or similar computer (a minicomputer, for instance). Thanks to the intelligence inherent in each of the LAN's PC clients, the division of labor between the client and the server reduces the amount of data that's sent through the network, boosting performance.

Client-server LANs, by allowing servers to be redesigned for specialized purposes, are responsible for most of the advances of the last decade:

- Equipment—Servers are detailed in Chapter 3, Hardware, and the devices that direct traffic around the network are described in Chapter 4, Cabling and Connections.
- Applications—New ways to achieve efficiency make up Chapter 5, LAN Applications, and the construction of globe-spanning networks is treated in Chapter 6, Internetworking.

- LAN Management—This new job category is the subject matter of Chapters 7 and 8, LAN Administration and LAN Security.
- The New Office—The "reengineering" of work itself is discussed in Chapter 9, The Networked Workplace.

The Two Architectures Compared

Both peer-to-peer and client-server networks provide much-needed connectivity to users, but they do so in different ways. Your selection of one network architecture over another may depend as much on how you do business as on what you can afford.

The dilemma: flexibility vs. control.

The nondedicated servers of the peer-to-peer LAN allow for more flexibility. Users can make resources available on their machines as necessary. To share a file with another user, one might make one's machine a server, which the other user could log in to and use the hard drive. On the other hand, with many servers on the network it can be harder to administer all the resources that are available. Backing up all the shared data, setting up security to guard network resources and just setting up who can use what resource on the network becomes more complicated. Another drawback is that nondedicated servers often suffer some performance drop as they are being used for two purposes at the same time: the user on the machine using the PC as a workstation and the other users on the network sharing the PC's resources.

Peer-to-peer networks are generally considered to be more democratic. That is, each user, whose computer is both a user and a provider of network services, has a responsibility for controlling his or her resources, just as does everyone else on the network. This makes sharing of information easier, but it can also make tracking of information more difficult. When it comes to backing up critical files, you might now have to schedule routine backups for most, if not all, users' workstations rather than for just one central server.

The dedicated servers used in client-server LANs are easier to administer, since all data is in one place. They are also faster, since they don't have a local user to serve. On the other hand, it is harder to make resources available on an ad hoc basis, since setting up a server is more difficult and time consuming.

Client-server networks lend themselves more to centralized administration, since the server is where all the important data and procedures are stored. User accounts are also defined at the server, not the client, making security more centralized than with peer-to-peer networks.

Major Network Operating Systems

The major systems software products include these:

Novell NetWare. The leading network operating system is available in several versions.

NetWare 2.2 is still available, primarily for small LANs not requiring many of the new features found in either NetWare 3.x or 4.x. Of these three versions, NetWare 2.2 is the one version of NetWare that can run on an 80286-based server, although performance is much less efficient than that on 80386- or 80486-based servers running NetWare 3.11 or 4.0. Novell does not plan to further develop NetWare 2.2, so it's a dead end, but we mention it for the sake of completeness.

NetWare 3.11 supports 5-, 10-, 50-, 100- and 250-user networks. It provides user transparent connectivity, internetworking capabilities, multiple remote connections, LAN-to-host communications, data protection, resource accounting, security and fault tolerance. It also includes accounting functions for charging for network use and tools for independent software developers.

NetWare 3.11 runs in protected mode on 80386-based or better file servers. It supports up to 250 users on one server, handling up to 32 terabytes of virtual disk space and 10,000 concurrent open files. The product allows file exchange between Macintosh, DOS and OS/2 users.

NetWare for Macintosh 3.11 brings Macintosh workstations into a NetWare network. Users can share files between Macintosh and DOS workstations.

NetWare 4.01 is a newly redesigned version of NetWare that supports up to 1,000 users on a server and also simplifies the grouping of users and access to network services. NetWare 4.01 offers many features that are appealing to users and managers of large LANs.

NetWare Lite 1.1 is a simple peer-to-peer, resource-sharing network operating system. It provides network management, messaging and local hard drive sharing capabilities. The product supports Novell's IPX protocol, allowing it to coexist with NetWare 2.2 and 3.11.

Artisoft LANtastic. The popular, low-cost, peer-to-peer network package provides printer, disk, CD-ROM and file sharing, e-mail, and local and network disk backup. Versions are available for DOS-, Macintosh-, Windows- and Unix-based LANs.

IBM PC Network Program. IBM's peer-to-peer network program works with IBM's broadband or token-ring network hardware.

Microsoft LAN Manager 2.0. This is a high-end network operating system, similar to NetWare, that provides a foundation for client-server computing and tools for complete LAN administration. It takes advantage of OS/2's multitasking functions, interprocess communications and built-in memory protection. The product includes facilities that let multiple servers be administered as single servers.

IBM LAN Server 3.0. This network operating system is based on Microsoft LAN Manager. It supports an unlimited number of subnetworks or domains and includes the ability to replicate data across multiple servers. The product supports 32-bit OS/2 and up to 1,000 clients on a single network.

Microsoft Windows for Workgroups. Windows for Workgroups 3.1 is a peer-to-peer network operating system that extends basic Windows utilities, including File Manager, Clipboard and Print Manager. It offers e-mail, scheduling and a sharable ClipBook. Administrative tools include WinMeter (which graphically shows percentage of CPU time used for local applications and resource sharing) and NetWatcher (which shows names of users connected to local PC, directories connected to and files opened).

Banyan VINES 5.0. This is a network operating system for local or global internetworking and management of PCs, minicomputers and mainframes. Support is available for DOS, Windows, OS/2 and the Macintosh.

Microsoft Windows NT. This new operating system is Microsoft's latest technology (NT stands for New Technology) for centralized servers and high-powered workstations. It's designed to be used on a variety of computing platforms, not just Intel-based computers. In addition to supporting 32-bit addressing for applications (enabling them to use over 4 gigabytes of RAM), Windows NT includes built-in networking support, a high-performance filing system and support for multiple processors in a single computer. Two versions are available, one for workstations, another for servers.

The Seven OSI Levels of LAN Design

The Open Systems Interconnection (OSI) Reference Model lies at the heart of every modern LAN. The OSI model was developed by the International Standards Organization to define a standard communication procedure for LANs. It allows hardware and software from different manufacturers to coexist harmoniously on a single LAN. It's not essential to fully understand the OSI model, any more than a driver needs to know the cyclic process of an internal combustion engine. But a basic knowledge of the OSI model helps you understand how a LAN operates and can be valuable when troubleshooting problems or adding new equipment to the network. And it appears in descriptions later in this book.

The OSI Reference Model can be used to compare how different network protocols work and how they can be related to each other. If you know how your network's protocols relate to the OSI Reference Model, you'll have a good basis for planning network expansion as well as understanding problems with your network.

The OSI Reference Model promotes flexibility in network operating systems because the model's specifications promote ready substitution of protocols within a layer. The model states what information must be passed between layers, but not how the information is generated by the protocols within a layer. This allows a developer to substitute better, newer or more efficient protocols within a layer without having to rewrite the protocols in other layers.

The OSI model is arranged into seven layers, as shown in Figure 2-1. Each layer performs a specific task and is built on the layers below it.

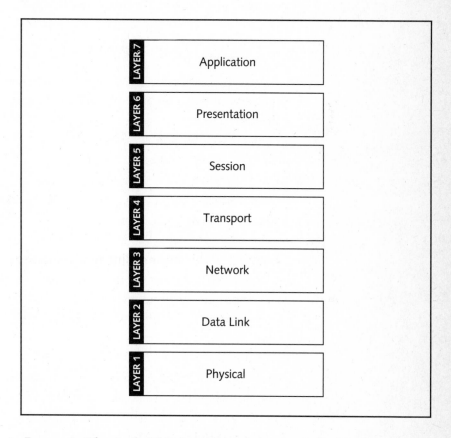

Figure 2-1
The OSI Model

Layer 1, Physical. This base layer is concerned with the physical connection between the PC and LAN, in other words, the cables, connectors, voltages, data transmission speed and other physical concerns. The protocols in this layer determine how the medium is used to transmit the data.

Layer 2, Data Link. This layer handles the network access-control mechanism—the little packets of information that make up LAN data. It controls each step that the data must take to get to the desired destination.

Layer 3, Network. Network switching, routing and management is the task of this layer. Its protocols determine what route the data must follow to get to the partner.

Layer 4, Transport. This layer handles network addressing and makes sure that data arrives safely and intact at the proper location. Protocols in this layer are responsible for determining where the partner is located on the network.

Layer 5, Session. This layer functions as an application interface to the transport layer. This is where the network determines who your partners are, i.e., who is supposed to receive the data.

Layer 6, Presentation. Providing a way for software applications to join the network is the function of this layer. Certain functions of the operating system, such as file redirection, are handled at this layer. Protocols in this layer determine what the data actually looks like.

Layer 7, Application. Network applications, including parts of the operating system and utilities, are handled at this layer. This is where your program determines what data it wants to send to the destination (or partner).

3 / Hardware

Some of the basic ingredients of a local area network are devices with which you may already be familiar. Others may be new to you. Let's go through the main elements of a local area network, one at a time, beginning with the basic engines of the system, the servers.

Servers are one of the major reasons for using a network. In general, a server is a hardware-software combination that provides a particular service to networked users, such as file sharing or modem sharing. There are five major types of servers that can be installed on a network:

File Servers store files that can be shared by everyone connected to the LAN. Though they may be ordinary PCs, in larger LANs they are special computers with lots of memory, huge disk drives and specialized software. In peer-to-peer LANs, any PC in the system can be a file server depending on the software it runs (as discussed in the previous chapter). The file server's hard disk contains the network operating system software, along with most of its application programs and user data. File servers work on a shared-file model, where file reads and writes by multiple users are interpreted by the server and then coordinated with other users' requests before being written to disk.

Database Servers may consist of hardware, software, or both. Any machine that stores a database on disk accessible to multiple users may be considered a database server. But the most useful ones have specialized database software using client-server architecture. Database servers don't share files, they share data. Instead of users performing a database search on their own machines (as with file-server-based databases), they ask the database server to do the search and send back only the requested data.

A file server is a computer that both stores files and controls how users can share its files on a network.

The client component runs on one or more LAN workstations, provides the user interface and allows people to ask for information or modify records in the database. The server component, running on a central machine, actually stores and controls the data—protecting it, granting access to multiple users, updating and deleting records on disk and perhaps communicating with other servers that also store pertinent data.

Because it separates the database function into two different segments, client-server design means that individual workstations can run a variety of different front ends—customized spreadsheets, query languages, etc.—and still retrieve information from the common database.

Print Servers provide LAN users with access to a centralized printer or a workstation's shared printer. Users send their printer output to the print server, which then temporarily stores each print job until it is printed. Jobs are usually handled in the order received, but some can be given priority and bumped to the head of the line.

Print servers allow fewer printers to satisfy more users and are also especially useful for expensive laser or high-speed printers, since they spread the cost of these machines over many users.

Fax Servers combine a LAN-connected PC with a fax board or external fax modem and software, allowing access to fax services by all users in the system. This way, any workstation on the LAN can send faxes. Some fax servers are self-contained, connecting directly to the network without requiring a PC.

Communications Servers allow users to pool or combine modems so that they can either dial out of the network to other offices or information sources, or, if they're remote users, dial in to the network to access other services on it. In either case, communications servers reduce the need for personal modems by making it easier to share communication hardware and software; they can usually route a waiting user from a busy modem in the pool to the next available modem, making communications more efficient.

The rest of this chapter will discuss servers in more detail, then describe other hardware that goes into a LAN.

File Servers (and Database Servers)

A file server is a computer that both stores files and controls how users can share its files on a network. It is a combination of hardware and software that allows LAN users to share computer programs and data. Often, though not always, a file server has significantly more data storage capacity than other computers on the network. It might also have more memory, several printers and modems attached and a tape backup capacity.

File servers come in all shapes and sizes. In some cases, only the software distinguishes a file server from a regular LAN workstation computer. For example, a regular PC may be a LAN file server if it runs software that allows other network users to communicate with it and use its hard disks. More often, companies install faster, more powerful machines for file servers because they are better able to serve many users at the same time. (The same is true for database servers.)

File server software is the part of the network operating system that offers a computer's hardware resources to other users on the LAN. It accepts incoming requests from LAN users, decides if they have permission to read or write files and sends a copy of a file's contents to the user when necessary. Users connect to a server by mounting ("mapping") a local logical drive to the file server's physical drive. That is, users access the file server's physical drive as if it were one of their local drives, using a designated drive letter, say F:. (Mac users see a new icon representing the server's disk on their desktop.) Their application programs work the same way as with locally stored files. The network operating system routes traffic to and from the proper file server hard disk when users request data from files stored on the server.

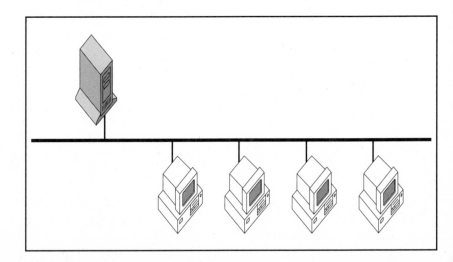

Figure 3-1 A Network File Server and Workstations

Performance

Many factors affect the performance of a file server. These include the speed of the network interface card, the type and length of cable, the efficiency of the network software, the type of application being run, the number of users on the network and the amount of RAM available. Probably the most important factor is the speed of the hard disk.

Most high-performance file servers include a very fast, and usually very large, hard disk. The access time is the time required to get data off the disk. In general, an access time of less than 20 milliseconds is very good for a file server hard disk; under 10ms is even better. Usually average access time is all you need to know when buying a server hard disk. Larger hard disks generally are faster than smaller ones.

One often overlooked aspect of the file server hard disk drive is its controller. Debates rage over which controller is better: standard IDE, ESDI (Enhanced Small Device Interface) or SCSI (Small Computer System Interface). Each has different advantages—price, speed and expandability, respectively. The tradeoff you make depends on your application and finances. An "intelligent" hard disk controller can cache frequently used data for faster access, so the microprocessor on the computer doesn't have to process every data transfer involving the disk. Though it adds cost, the upgraded disk controller provides enormous performance improvements.

Performance is not the only question to think about when installing a file server hard disk. Capacity is crucial. It's hard to get too much data storage on a file server; a general rule is to get twice the amount you think you need. Since LANs always grow, expandability is also important. File servers should be large enough to accommodate more disk drives as they are needed.

Most file servers are larger and faster than most network workstations. Vendors now recommend at least an 80486-based file server. In addition, system clock speeds of 50MHz and higher are becoming popular. File servers with this type of hardware are faster than ordinary desktop PCs running at 20MHz or 25MHz. The performance advantages usually justify the added cost.

Fault Tolerance

While performance is probably the most important factor when buying a file server, reliability is also crucial. Here is where fault tolerance comes in. Fault tolerance is the general name given to any scheme designed to prevent data loss from events like power failures, disk crashes, electromagnetic interference and disk controller failure. One form of fault tolerance is to read data immediately after it's been written to the disk, verifying that what was placed on the disk was correct. Some file server software does this.

Transaction tracking goes a bit further than this. It groups operations on the network into transactions and remembers each transaction until it's completed. All operations within a transaction must be complete or none of them are registered by the server. If the file server is interrupted during a transaction, transaction tracking returns the file server back to its state before the transaction. This is especially useful if a database is being updated when something happens. Transaction tracking can also increase performance by grouping updates together, keeping all disk access requests together so they may be done at the same time.

Two more types of fault tolerance are disk mirroring and disk duplexing. In disk mirroring, one hard disk controller writes to and reads from two hard disks located in the same computer. If one hard disk should fail, the other can be used, since it is an exact replica. However, if the controller fails, both disks will be corrupted. Disk duplexing takes care of this by using two disk controllers and two hard disks in the same computer. Disk duplexing has several advantages, though it is more expensive. First, a controller problem will not corrupt all data. Second, though the two controllers ultimately have the same data, they need not do the same thing at the same time. While one is writing data, the other may be reading it, thereby speeding overall performance.

An extension of disk duplexing is called shadowing. Here, a second file server, also attached to the network, receives all the data of the first. Should the first file server fail, the second file server may take over. This is one of the most expensive forms of fault tolerance, but it helps LAN users recover from a broken file server more quickly than any other method. Shadowing is used in downtime-sensitive situations, where loss of the file server for more than a few minutes can be devastating.

- *Transaction tracking*
- *Disk mirroring*
- *Disk duplexing*

Recently, a new form of disk system has been used to provide fast, reliable performance at a lower cost. In this system, called a disk array or RAID (Redundant Array of Inexpensive Disks), multiple drives are grouped together into what appears to be a single logical volume, but the component drives work in parallel for faster data access. Data redundancy, or storing copies of the data on multiple disks within the array, improves the reliability of the array. Most disk arrays use some form of striping, where alternating segments of a file are written first to one drive and then to the second drive (or to two parts of the same disk), increasing the chances that at least some of the data will be intact after a disk crash. Also, as mentioned previously, RAID disks can be mirrored.

RAIDs are classified from level 0 to level 5 according to the type of data redundancy they employ (see Table 3-1). RAID level 0, the lowest level of redundancy, uses data striping on a single disk, while RAID 4 alternates writing data sectors onto different disks and uses one entire disk for storing data for data correction and recovery. Level 5, the highest level, follows the same procedures as level 4 arrays, but distributes the check data over multiple disks for better throughput and reliability.

Table 3-1 RAID Levels

Level	Data Striping	Disk Mirroring	Error Correction	Comments
0	●			Data written across multiple disks
1	●	●		Data written twice, once to disk, once to disk mirror
2	●		●	Has no mirror disk, must rebuild failed disk
3	●		●	Error correction in drive-controller hardware, including parity drive
4	●		●	Performs simultaneous reads from different drives
5	●		●	Entirely in software; stripes data and parity across array

Print Servers

One of the common reasons to install a LAN is to share computer peripherals, including large hard disks and printers. Sharing printers means that only one PC needs to have printers attached to it. Other users send their print jobs, documents, spreadsheets and reports to this print server. The print server machine handles all the printing requirements for the group of users. This can save money and make printing easier and faster. For a print server to handle many jobs coming in at the same time, it must have something called a spool. Spool is an acronym for Simultaneous Peripheral Operation On Line, but nobody ever says that.

A spool is a combination of RAM and disk space that stores printing files while the printer is busy. This way, print jobs can be stored in the spool while the printer is working on another job. Most of the time, print jobs are spooled to a hard disk at the print server where they join a queue, waiting to be printed in a first-in, first-out order as the printer becomes ready. Most print servers allow users to assign priorities to their print jobs so the higher-priority jobs can be moved up to the head of the queue and lower-priority jobs can be held for printing later.

LAN Printing

In general, LAN printing works as follows. Software in the user's machine captures the printed information and sends it over the network. The application that is running, say, a word processor, acts as if it were printing a document locally, but the print software steps in to redirect the output over the network.

At the print server, software handles the incoming print job. If the printer is free, the document may be printed immediately. If the printer is not free, the document is stored in a print file—spooled— on the print server's hard disk. The file also joins the queue, waiting its turn to be sent to the printer.

Spooling may be done for two reasons. First, the printer is busy, so the print server must store the file until the printer can take it. Second, the printer is not fast enough to process the whole file at once, so the server stores the last parts of the file while the first parts print.

The print server also has a buffer. The buffer, a chunk of memory, is used to feed print jobs to the printer at the correct pace. Data waiting to be printed is stored in the buffer just before it is sent. The larger the buffer, the faster the printing, since fewer accesses to disk are necessary to print the file.

This points out the difference between a spool and a buffer. A spool is a software-hardware combination that stores the files for printing and then sends them when ready. A buffer is a chunk of memory that holds the data while the printer and PC communicate. Both improve the performance of LAN printing.

Print Problems

One of the most common problems that crops up when trying to print on a network is conflict between the application and the network. If the application talks to the printer port directly, the network operating system does not have the opportunity to redirect the output. This type of problem occurs more often when printing to serial ports than to parallel ports. It is easier to handle a serial port than a parallel port; therefore more applications leave parallel operations to DOS. The solution, where possible, is to configure the application to use the parallel port, so that the network can more easily redirect the file.

Another problem occurs when the application has its own print spool. Again, the application checks the hardware directly to see when to send data, bypassing the network spool. The solution is to disable the application's spool.

A third LAN printing problem is caused by multiple print buffers. Besides the print server, the application, the PC, the network and the printer may all have print buffers, too. Sometimes, disruptions happen while one buffer waits for another. The solution is to use only one buffer. Performance is not hurt significantly and memory resources are conserved.

A fourth LAN printing problem comes when multiple users share one printer, each user setting the printer with different fonts, character widths, line spacing, etc. Once a user is finished, the printer may be stuck with that user's settings. Some applications allow users to send printer control codes; so do some network operating systems and some LAN printing utilities (see below). These codes can be used to reset a printer after every print job. This way, all users know that the printer is starting with the same settings no matter who has used it previously.

Unfortunately, in some cases the printer control codes used by a particular application may interfere with network operations or with network printer control codes. For example, the network operating system may misinterpret a printer control code from the application as a printer release code and disconnect the user from the printer. Another symptom of such conflicts is garbled printing. Only trial and error can eliminate these problems. Most likely the application must be reconfigured not to use the printer control code commands. Those of the network operating system or a printer utility must be used instead.

The last set of printing problems is unavoidable. Multiple users have multiple requirements for paper, but most printers can only hold one type of paper at a time. One way to cope is to have more than one shared printer, each using different paper. If this is too expensive or inappropriate, some kind of notification needs to be implemented when users switch paper. E-mail is probably the best tool for this. With e-mail notification, users will not send print jobs to printers with the wrong paper installed. Some network operating systems handle forms automatically, notifying operators when paper changes are needed. Some printer utilities can also serve this purpose.

Utilities

Virtually all network operating systems support some kind of LAN printing. However, the variation in features is great and some are inconvenient. Some network operating systems require the user to leave a particular application before setting up the print process; the user must explicitly tell the network operating system to be on the lookout for a print job and then tell it when the job is over. Other network operating systems require that all shared printers be attached to a file server, which is especially inconvenient when file servers are locked up for security purposes. Finally, many network operating systems do not allow network users to send printer control codes to network printers.

Several LAN printing utilities exist to solve these problems. Usually pop-up programs that may be called up while another application is being used, they allow users to control the printer and print server from their own PCs without quitting what they are doing. Users may manipulate the print queue, check on which files have been spooled, choose printing codes, send jobs, reconfigure the printer and perform many other tasks all without leaving their application.

When any PC can act as a print server, printers may be placed conveniently throughout a LAN.

Many printing utilities have the ability to automate printer configuration. A printing utility can send printer control codes to reset the printer default configuration after every print job. This way, every user knows how the printer is set before using it.

Many LAN printing utilities also allow any PC on the network to act as a print server. These utilities are really additions to the network operating system, since they are fundamentally enhancing its operation. When any PC can act as a print server, printers may be placed conveniently throughout a LAN.

Another useful feature of many printing utilities is print notification. Users are notified when their print jobs have finished printing, a terrific convenience if the printer is out of earshot. Another good feature is the ability to standardize line feeds and form feeds so users don't have to do this manually. This reduces the chance that users will go to the printer and change it, or leave it offline.

Network printers have their own special features and are discussed later in this chapter along with other peripheral devices.

Fax Servers

Facsimile machines have become as essential as the telephone. But frankly, we're all tired of waiting for the fax machine to free up, and we're tired of paper jams. Fax boards are the next stage. Fax boards fit into a slot in a PC and enable users to send faxes to any other fax machine or fax board anywhere. They eliminate the need to print out a computer file to fax it. On the receiving end, they save fax paper because the message can be printed out if needed but can be saved as a graphics file.

What makes all this possible is the fax server. The fax board still only resides in one PC on the LAN, but the fax server software lets all users access its services. Giving a LAN fax capability has two advantages: accessibility and speed.

One reason for sharing a peripheral is making it accessible to many users. Faxes are no different. Both fax machines and fax boards are limited to a single location. That's a real pain if that location is on the other side of the building. Fax servers change that, since any workstation on the LAN can send a fax. The fax server effectively places a virtual fax machine on every desktop.

The fax server's second justification is that it's faster than either a fax board or fax machine. The speed doesn't come from a higher transmission rate (that's standardized), but from avoiding so many steps: There's no printing of the file, no walking to the fax machines, no waiting in line. Just compose the fax, select the recipient's fax phone number and it's off. The software takes care of the rest.

The one major drawback to fax boards and fax servers is that the document to be sent must already be in a computer. Consider investing in a scanner if you need to transmit documents that are already on paper. With the scanner, a LAN has all the links of a truly paperless office.

There are three ways to implement a fax server. The first is with remote control software. With this, the networked user temporarily takes control of the PC housing the fax board. It's as if the user's computer were actually the fax server. With control of the fax PC, all operations at the host become available at the remote workstation. When a fax is not being transmitted, that PC can be used as a normal workstation.

This works best if the fax board can work without interrupting the computer's microprocessor, so the user doesn't have to stop working every time someone on the LAN sends a fax. The remote control approach has drawbacks. Users have to learn more about controlling the fax software; moreover, only one PC can control the server at a time.

A second method is setting up a fax server, which can often double as a file server or print server on the LAN. In other instances, it is a distinct machine dedicated as a communication or facsimile server. Fax servers enable multiple users to send faxes simultaneously, avoiding the major drawback of communication software. They can use a dedicated PC or their own hardware. And those using their own hardware have the benefit of speed and simplicity.

The third method is tied to an existing e-mail system, treating faxes as simply another form of e-mail message. However, instead of being sent to a user's computer, they are sent to the fax gateway. The address includes the phone number to be dialed. The fax gateway strips away e-mail codes and sends the fax on its way. This approach is great if an e-mail system is already installed. Users familiar with the e-mail will have little to learn: They send the fax to the fax computer, and the software handles the rest. Once the document is sent, the user is notified through the e-mail system.

Fax servers are not without drawbacks. For example, there is still no standard way to distribute incoming faxes without having someone read them to figure out their intended destination. And to fax documents that are already on paper, a fax server is of no use without a scanner to put that paper document into electronic form. As we move further towards electronic media, fax servers will become more relevant.

Communications (Dial-in) Servers

Just as LAN users can share a fax modem, communications servers provide shared modem services to LAN users. The idea is simple: Rather than connect a modem to each user's PC, attach a communications server to the LAN and attach a few modems to the communications server. Then, when someone needs to use a modem, the system redirects the user's modem commands to the communications server, which then selects the next available modem in its pool.

Communications servers can also provide an additional advantage, that of remote access to the network. With the increasing number of users taking notebooks and laptop computers on the road to do their jobs, it's becoming more important to provide them with access to the network back at the office. A communications server with modems connected to multiple phone lines can provide incoming callers with ready access to the network and fewer busy signals.

Communications servers usually work in conjunction with a software driver installed on the user's PC. This driver redirects any commands or data sent to a port (COM1, for example) and sends the data over the network to the communications server. The server then uses the commands and data to control one of its attached modems to complete the link. As far as the user's telecom program and operating system are concerned, the networked modem is just as good as a locally attached one.

When looking to install a dial-in server, here are a few key issues to keep in mind:

- How many modems do you want to support? Some dial-in servers support only 1 modem, while others can handle as many as 16.

- Will you need to support more than one network protocol? TCP/IP, IPX and AppleTalk are the most common protocols supported.

- What kind of security do you want to implement? At a minimum, dial-in servers support user names and passwords to restrict access; some models also include a call-back option that hangs up and dials the user's modem at a prearranged number.

- Do you want to monitor usage? A few dial-in servers offer the ability to log both incoming and outgoing calls.

In closing, if you're planning to install a dial-in server, you should be aware that these devices are only available for Ethernet and LocalTalk; no one has yet released a token-ring version.

Optical Disks

Magnetic disks aren't the only mass storage devices out there. Optical disks are enjoying increasing popularity. Optical disks use reflected light instead of magnetic pulses to store data. They use a controller, but where a hard disk drive has several disks, an optical disk only has one. They're also removable and interchangeable.

Optical disks are a little slower than regular magnetic disks, but the sacrifice in time is more than made up for in volume and durability. Optical disks are made of an extremely hard, resilient plastic. They can withstand all sorts of physical abuse. Furthermore, the information is chemically sealed onto the plastic and the optical beam never touches the surface, so there is no risk of head crashes.

Most optical disks used on LANs are write-once read-many, or WORM, drives. Files cannot be erased from WORM drives, so a complete trail of updates is kept. There's no such thing as accidentally erasing a file.

The newer type of optical disk is rewriteable. Just as with magnetic disks, files can be erased from these disks and the space used again. With multiple platter technology like the Jukebox, storage capacity can reach several gigabytes. The big advantage to optical disks is that they are far more reliable than regular magnetic disks.

Workstations

The most common type of LAN workstation is the standard IBM PC, PS/2 or compatible machine. In many cases, those machines were already installed as single-user systems before the network was installed. With these PCs, users retain control over their own machines, using network storage and printing resources as they become necessary.

Standalone PCs and compatibles used as workstations also provide flexibility in case of changes in the network (and during emergencies in which the network file server is temporarily unavailable). Their expandability, power and independence—the same characteristics that have made general-purpose microcomputers so popular—make PC workstations well suited for networking in companies where users' computing needs vary greatly. While some users might use their network workstations for word processing only (and could get by with inexpensive PCs), most users need 80386- or 80486-based workstations for most contemporary software.

In choosing PC workstations, keep ease of installation and maintenance in mind. The more different types of machines on the network, the more different software configurations the network will require, and the greater the likelihood of incompatible combinations of CPUs and expansion cards. Try to strike a balance between standardizing network installations and installing customized hardware designed for individual users' needs. Also, watch out for the hidden cost of hooking up leftover PCs as a way to save money on individual workstations. Older machines may have outdated, inefficient network interface cards. It can become difficult to find people who know how to set their switches or troubleshoot these 80286 computers. The latest level of software, moreover, may not work on an old machine. A mixed network may need two versions of the same software for different workstations, which may ultimately be incompatible.

The more different types of machines on the network, the more different software configurations.

A popular alternative to buying complete, standalone PCs for use as network workstations is buying specialized network nodes. Typically, a low-cost workstation resembles a standard PC, except that it lacks disk drives and is limited in its expansion capabilities. Often called diskless workstations, these inexpensive PC nodes don't need bays for disk drives, and so can be built smaller and lighter than their standalone cousins. They can range from 386SX-based machines—suitable for word processing, database or spreadsheet processing—to powerful 486- or Pentium-based workstations with high-resolution graphics capabilities built in.

An important advantage of diskless workstations is their added security in a networked environment. Because copying sensitive data from the network to a floppy disk is impossible, the network administrator can control who copies files to and from the network. Some "diskless" workstations include a hard disk controller but not a floppy drive, enabling users to operate locally on the PC—without relying completely on the network file server—but preventing users from copying data to floppy disks without permission. Network security is treated in more detail in Chapter 8, LAN Security.

Peripheral Devices

One of the main reasons for installing a LAN is to give users access to a wide range of peripheral devices. Virtually any peripheral that can be used with a standalone PC can also find a home on a LAN. Let's look at some of these units.

Printers

Laser printers have become standard LAN peripherals over the past few years. The newest units offer a 600 dots-per-inch output resolution and an 8 pages-per-minute or faster print speed. PostScript and TrueType support are also important features.

Although laser printers have largely replaced dot matrix printers, several types of "alternative" printers are still viable network choices. Most important among these are ink-jet printers, which deliver laser-quality output at lower cost, although they can be quite slow. Some types of ink-jet printers can also produce color output.

With the advent of faster laser printers, some vendors have started to offer printers that have the network interface built directly into them. In particular, these network printers are aimed at the Ethernet market. Their built-in processors receive and process printing data directly from the network and pass it on to the printer at speeds faster than that found in print servers. One reason for this is that network printers do not have to deal with the slower data transmission speeds of serial or parallel ports to send data to a printer.

Scanners

As noted earlier, scanners can be used to input paper-based data into a computer. The technology is called optical character recognition (OCR). Scanners can also be used to digitize photographs, graphic images or entire documents into a computer-usable form.

Sturdy flatbed scanners are most commonly used on LANs, although handheld models are also gaining popularity. Users can select between monochrome and color scanner models.

Backup Units

One of the most important tasks for any computer user is backing up data to preserve it against accidental loss, system crashes and other disasters. When data is meant to be shared, as on a network, backup becomes even more important. Networks can make it easier to backup data, either by the user or at the request of the system administrator.

The simplest approach to backing up local user data is to copy all data to a file server, and let the system administrator back up the server's files. A similar approach is to provide a backup server, which is usually a computer on the network with a tape drive or similar large-capacity storage medium attached to it. Users can then employ backup software to schedule regular backups of their files to that server as necessary. This latter method is preferred, since users know their data is being backed up and don't have to depend on a system administrator to back up a server.

But if users aren't very regular about backing up their files (and many aren't), some vendors offer software that allows the system administrator to schedule backups of workstations at either a file server or a tape backup unit on the network. Often, these system-wide backups are scheduled for the wee hours of the morning, when users aren't usually on the network.

When shopping for backup software or a backup server, be sure to find one that includes automatic scheduling of backups as well as selective restoration of files that have been backed up. Also, in a large network with many users and large files, consider drives that include a carousel of tapes or WORM disks.

Other Peripherals

Modems, CD-ROM drives, pen plotters and tape drives are just a few of the many other peripherals that can be added to a LAN.

4 / Cabling and Connections

Cabling
Wireless LANs
Topologies
Connecting Devices

Now that we've introduced the hardware in a LAN, it's time to consider how it all hooks together. Before we go on to a detailed discussion, let's preview the basic elements required to connect up all the parts of a LAN.

Though it may seem to be the simplest component on a LAN, cabling can be the most expensive part, in some cases making up 50 percent of the total cost. Cabling can also be the largest source of network problems both in installation and maintenance. For these reasons, cabling should be taken very seriously. Cabling can be twisted-pair, coaxial, twinaxial or fiber-optic.

Interface cards are printed circuit boards that fit in the expansion chassis of a computer to make the physical connection with the LAN cable. The interface card is responsible for getting raw data from the computer onto the network and vice versa. This requires translation from parallel to serial form and back, buffering, packet creation, encoding/decoding, cable access, and transmission and reception.

Repeaters are network devices that amplify and regenerate network signals so that LANs can be connected over longer distances.

Bridges are devices that connect different LANs, allowing communication between devices on separate cabling systems. Bridges are used to connect LANs with different hardware and different protocols. They keep networks manageable by allowing a department to connect several small networks rather than create one large, unwieldy network. This reduces traffic for individual computers and improves network performance.

Bridges are related to but differ from other devices like routers, which determine the best way to forward data toward its correct destination, connecting LANs with the same protocols but different hardware; and gateways, which connect two LANs with different protocols by translating between them.

Here are more details on some of these components.

Cabling

Cabling is the medium used in most networks to connect devices. Its ability to transmit encoded signals allows it to carry data from one place to another. These signals might be electrical, as in copper cable, or optical, as in fiber-optic cable.

A few networks don't use cable. They use radio, microwave or infrared signals to transmit and receive data. These networks are usually more expensive and less reliable, but they can operate where cable is inappropriate, say, across a river or freeway.

Most networks use copper cable because it has the right electrical properties to transmit information over distance. Such electrical properties as resistance, shielding and flexibility differ from cable type to cable type (see Figure 4-1). Understanding these differences helps the user choose the right cable.

For LAN users today there are three basic cable types to choose from—coaxial, twisted-pair and fiber-optic. Each has certain advantages and disadvantages. While the majority of installed LANs use coaxial cable, twisted-pair cable has become very popular, and fiber-optic cable's use is growing.

Figure 4-1 Typical Cable Construction

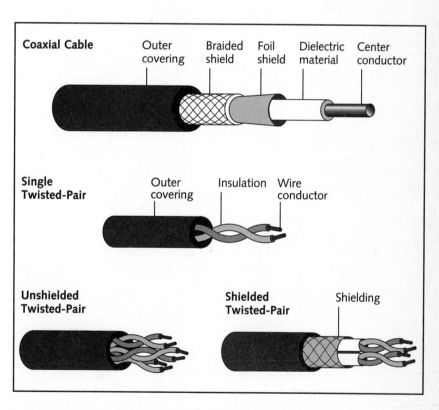

Originally, network protocols like Ethernet and ARCnet were designed to run only on coaxial cable. These protocols have been around the longest, explaining why the majority of installed LANs use coaxial cable. Recently, however, these protocols have been modified to run on twisted-pair and fiber-optic cable. The same is true for other protocols, including token ring. The result is that access method no longer determines cable type.

One common rule to remember about cable is that there is often a tradeoff between speed and distance. This is especially true of copper cables. It is possible to increase the speed of data transmission on a cable, but in doing so the distance that data can travel is usually reduced. Devices like repeaters and amplifiers can help here, but the physical properties of the cable impose certain limits.

Coaxial Cable

Coaxial cable consists of four parts. The core is the inner conductor, a solid metal wire. It is surrounded by the second layer, insulation. The third layer, a thin tubular metal screen, surrounds the insulation. Its axis of curvature coincides with that of the inner conductor (hence the term coaxial). The outermost layer is a plastic cover that surrounds the rest.

If you have cable TV, you already have coaxial cable.

Coaxial cable has been around the longest of any data transmission cable. If you have cable TV, you already have coaxial cable. In fact, one type of Ethernet uses broadband transmission over coaxial cable, which is the same principle used by cable TV. Both take advantage of coaxial cable's ability to transmit many signals at the same time. In both cases, each signal is called a channel. Each channel travels along the cable using a different frequency so it doesn't interfere with other channels.

Coaxial cable has high bandwidth. This is another way of saying it can handle plenty of traffic, which is probably its biggest advantage. High bandwidth is also another way of saying high speed. That is, coaxial cable supports high-speed networking. Other advantages of coaxial cable include its relatively high immunity to interference, its ability to carry signals over significant distances and its familiarity to many LAN installers.

There are several sizes of coaxial cable. Standard Ethernet cable, also called thick Ethernet, is as thick as a finger. Newer Ethernet cable, often called Thinnet, resembles cable TV coaxial cabling. The thicker cable is more robust, harder to damage and transmits over longer distances. It's also harder to connect.

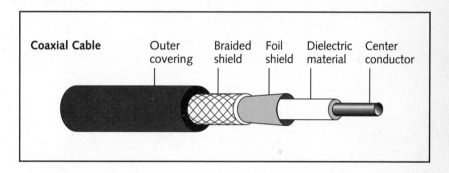

Figure 4-2
Coaxial Cable

Standard Ethernet coaxial cable requires something called a vampire tap and drop cable to connect to a LAN device. This combination is bulky and expensive. Thinnet uses something called a BNC connector that's easier to use, and Thinnet with BNC connectors is now the standard office coaxial cable.

The long-term experience with coaxial cable makes it a proven technology. "Coax" handles nearly every type of transmission, including video, voice and data. Twisted-pair cannot come close to this versatility, and fiber-optic cable is only beginning to.

Twisted-Pair Cable

Twisted-pair cable is an older product than coaxial cable, but it has not been used for carrying data at high speeds until recently. Instead, it has been carrying voice. It is used extensively in the nationwide telephone system. Practically every office building in the United States has twisted-pair cable installed in the walls.

In the past few years, however, vendors have figured out how to transmit data over twisted-pair cable at higher speeds. Token-ring networks, introduced in 1984, raised twisted-pair speed to 4Mbps. In 1987, several vendors introduced Ethernet on twisted-pair cable, raising the speed to 10Mbps. The maximum distance between computers for these types of networks, however, is much shorter than Ethernet on coaxial cable—about 300 feet compared to approximately 1,500 feet.

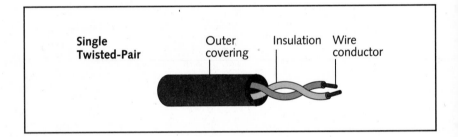

Figure 4-3 Basic Twisted-Pair Cable

Nevertheless, twisted-pair cable offers some significant benefits. It's lighter, thinner and more flexible than either coaxial or fiber-optic cable, thus easier to install. The cable is usually cheaper, although installation costs may be almost as high as for thin coaxial cable. Another advantage of twisted-pair cable is modular cabling. While modular cabling is now being developed in coaxial and fiber-optic environments, it is already common in the telephone industry's twisted-pair world. A modular cabling system, built with patch panels, wiring closets and common connector jacks, makes it easier to move computers without rewiring the LAN.

Among the many types of twisted-pair, the most important distinction is between shielded and unshielded. The former has an insulating material wrapped around the two twisted wires and the latter doesn't. Shielded cable is more immune to interference, which usually translates into higher speeds and longer distances and greater reliability. It is more expensive.

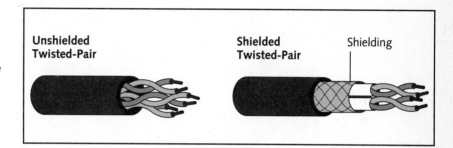

Figure 4-4 Unshielded vs. Shielded Twisted-Pair Cable

Twisted-pair makes sense in many installations. Its low cost, ease of use and flexibility make it ideal in offices or workgroups without heavy traffic or electromagnetic interference.

Fiber-Optic Cable

Fiber-optic cable is simple in design. There is a core fiber of standard diameter, measured in microns (1 micron is one-millionth of a meter). Surrounding this is a solid "cladding." Covering the cable is a protective layer. Originally, fiber-optic cable was made of glass. Plastic fibers have been introduced recently.

LEDs, or light emitting diodes, are used to send signals down a fiber-optic cable. A detector receives the signals and converts them back to electrical impulses. Signals are encoded into light in many ways. The most popular way is to vary the intensity.

There are two types of fiber-optic cable, single mode and multimode. Multimode is cheaper but doesn't carry the distance of single mode. In multimode fiber, the light bounces off the cable's internal walls as it travels down the cable. This causes the signal to weaken sooner. In single mode fiber, the light travels straight down the fiber. Single mode fiber-optic cable has a smaller diameter than multimode, making it harder to manufacture.

Fiber-optic cable has been touted as the answer to all the problems of copper cable. It is immune to electromagnetic interference, has enormous bandwidth, can carry data over huge distances and is suitable for voice, video and data. But it has not been embraced by many LAN users yet.

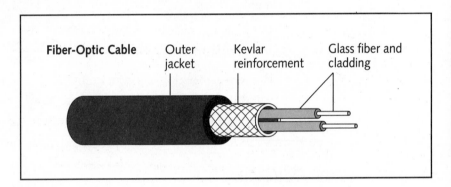

Figure 4-5
Fiber-Optic Cable

Fiber-optic connectors, though much easier to put on the cable than previously, are still more difficult to install than coaxial cable. The same is true with splicing fiber-optic cable, the most difficult part of fiber-optic installation.

Another problem is the lack of diagnostic tools for fiber-optic cable. Time domain reflectometers, ohmmeters, voltmeters and oscilloscopes can all be used to locate copper cable faults and diagnose cable conditions. Only a few similar tools exist for fiber-optic cable, making maintenance more difficult and more expensive. It is this lack of diagnostic tools, combined with the lack of knowledge, that makes LAN users wary of fiber-optic cable.

In the LAN arena, fiber has enjoyed its greatest success as a backbone medium used to connect LANs in different buildings. Its properties make it ideal for heavy traffic, rough environments and

Advantages: A cable break disables only one spoke of the network, limiting the disruption. Easy to locate cable breaks.

Disadvantages: Higher cost due to price of hub; although quite reliable, hubs are single-point-of-failure. Star LANs use plenty of cable.

Figure 4-6
LAN Topologies

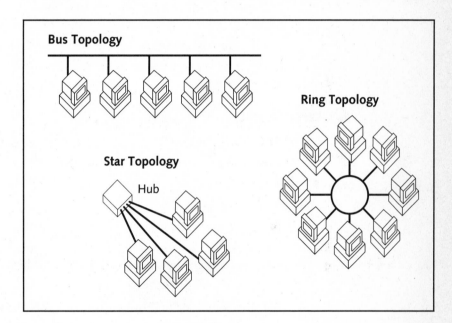

Ring Networks

Ring networks link computers and other nodes in a ringlike loop. As in a bus network, information passes from node to node. Unlike a bus LAN, each node features a repeater that amplifies the signal, allowing ring networks to cover very long geographical distances. A number of different fault-tolerance technologies allow ring LANs to keep functioning as usual in the event of a node or cable failure. FDDI and token-ring networks follow the ring topology.

Advantages: A compromise in cost between bus and star networks.

Disadvantages: The LAN slows down as more nodes are added.

Hybrids

Many users opt for hybrid LANs that take advantage of two or more topologies. This approach allows the LAN to meet the specific physical requirements of a particular office while providing the best returns in cost and performance.

Connecting Devices

Here are some other important components that can help you hook together your local area network and make it run more smoothly:

Hubs

A hub is a piece of hardware designed to be a central point for connecting cables together to form a network. It is usually a flat box about 2 to 6 inches high and 1 to 2 feet wide (depending on how much it can do), which costs anywhere from $500 to $2,500 and sits in the wiring closet.

With the advent of twisted-pair Ethernet, hubs have taken on a strategic role in networks. Twisted-pair Ethernet requires that a twisted-pair cable run from each node to a hub. The hub is responsible for amplifying and retransmitting the signal to the other cables connected to the hub (a hub is basically a multiport repeater). If the Ethernet hub breaks, the network stops functioning.

Since all network traffic passes through the hub, this device is an ideal location for monitoring network traffic and for performing diagnostics. Many network management schemes have evolved around the monitoring of Ethernet hubs (see Chapter 7, LAN Administration).

One difference between low-end hubs and the more expensive active or "smart" hubs is the amount of network management support that's built into the hub. Many smart hubs can perform network diagnostics online without intervention by the network manager. Alarms set for certain network problems can then be automatically relayed to the network manager when something goes wrong.

Repeaters

Repeaters are rather simple devices that amplify any electrical signal received on one port and retransmit the amplified signal out the other port, allowing greatly separated workstations to operate on the network. If some workstations are too far away from the rest of the network to stay within the length limits of the cabling being used, a repeater effectively extends the cable to link them to the rest of the network.

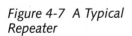

Figure 4-7 A Typical Repeater

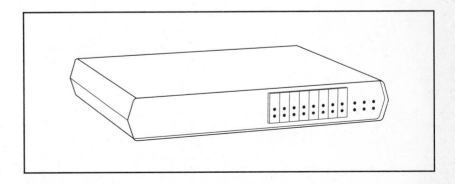

Repeaters have two limitations. First, a repeater has a lower limit on the strength of the signal that it can amplify, which limits one to no more than two repeaters per cable segment. Second, a repeater does not isolate traffic from one part of the network from traffic on another part of the network, so it does not reduce the number of collisions between packets. When the number of packet collisions causes the network to fail or slow to a crawl, the next step is to install a bridge.

Bridges

A bridge is a device that connects two similar networks. It takes packets from one network, retransmits them on the other network, and vice versa. While it does this, it regenerates the signal strength of the packets, allowing data to travel further. In this sense, a bridge is just like a repeater, but a bridge does more than a repeater because it isolates traffic on one LAN from traffic on another LAN.

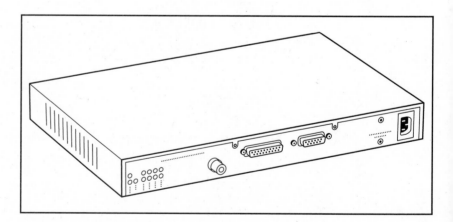

Figure 4-8 A Bridge

A bridge is intelligent. A bridge examines each packet as it passes, checking the source and destination addresses. If a packet coming from Station 1 on LAN A is destined for Station 5 on LAN B, the bridge redirects the packet onto LAN B. If a packet coming from Station 1 on LAN A is destined for Station 3 on LAN A, the bridge lets it go.

A bridge is also a piece of hardware, another little box that usually sits in the wiring closet. It's about the same size as a hub but more expensive: anywhere from $2,000 to $10,000. The higher price is because a bridge does more than connect. A bridge can maintain connections, amplify signals and has its own built-in microprocessor so it can know which workstations are on which part of the network.

A bridge simply passes packets back and forth, regardless of protocols, the way a telephone allows an English speaker to call someone in China even if the two people can't understand each other.

The most common reason to use bridges is that they improve performance by reducing the traffic on each LAN connected to the bridge. A bridge divides a large LAN into two smaller parts and keeps packets generated in one part from being transmitted to the second part unless the packets are addressed to a device there. This reduces the amount of traffic on each, while still allowing workstations on both segments to talk to each other.

It is possible that a poorly placed bridge can reduce performance by creating a bottleneck. However, it doesn't take too much effort to discover the best place to put a bridge. For example, it doesn't make sense to split up a workgroup of five or ten people who work closely together. A bridge between this workgroup and another workgroup, however, could improve performance dramatically. With the bridge, the two workgroups may still communicate transparently. Only communication between groups, not communication within groups, moves through the bridge.

Another reason to use a bridge is to change from one type of cable to another. For example, you may run twisted-pair cable in the offices and fiber-optic cable between buildings. Segments can be connected with a bridge, so "long distance" traffic can flow freely from one segment to another while local traffic stays local. Broadband and baseband Ethernet networks may be connected this way, too. The same thing goes for StarLAN and Ethernet. Or a 16Mbps token-ring backbone may use bridges to connect a number of local 4Mbps token-rings.

Bridges work at the data link layer of the OSI Reference Model. This means they can be used to interconnect LANs that use many different protocols. For example, the same bridge may connect networks running TCP/IP, DECnet, OSI, IPX and XNS protocols. But it does not allow one user "speaking" TCP/IP to talk to another user "speaking" IPX or OSI. A device that does that is called a gateway; it actually translates between protocols. A bridge simply passes packets back and forth, regardless of protocols, the way a telephone allows an English speaker to call someone in China even if the two people can't understand each other. A bridge does let any two users "speaking" the same protocol talk to each other.

Many networks have more than one protocol running on them. For example, two groups of Sun workstation users may use TCP/IP most of the time and OSI some of the time. A bridge between the groups passes both TCP/IP and OSI packets. The bridge doesn't know or care which protocol it is passing. The key thing to remember about the bridge is that the two machines on either side must use the same protocols to be connected usefully.

The most common standardized data-link layer protocols are Ethernet, token ring, and StarLAN. Ethernet-to-Ethernet is the most common bridge, followed by StarLAN-to-StarLAN and Ethernet-to-StarLAN. Ethernet-to-token ring bridges are also just appearing. Different network protocols produce different numbers of information bytes in each packet. So because the packet size used on the two networks is different, this is a more difficult bridge to implement.

Learning and Filtering

A bridge works with something called an address table. When a bridge is attached and plugged in, it begins to send out broadcasts asking for replies from all stations on the local segment of the network. As the stations return the broadcast, the bridge builds a table of local addresses. This process is called learning. Most bridges are learning bridges, though one or two (called static bridges) still force the LAN manager to enter all the local addresses.

Once the bridge has the local address table, it is ready to operate. When it receives a packet, it examines the source address (see Figure 4-6). If the packet's address is local, the bridge ignores it. If it is for another LAN, the bridge copies the packet onto the second LAN. Looking at the packet's address is called filtering. Copying the packet to the other side is called forwarding.

In a broadcast storm, a broadcast message is repeatedly copied across bridges until the network screeches to a halt.

The most basic type of filtering is keeping local packets local and sending remote packets to the other subnetwork. The next type is filtering based on specific source and destination addresses. For example, a bridge might stop one station from sending packets outside of its local LAN. Or a bridge might stop all "outside" packets destined for a particular station, thereby restricting the other stations with which it can communicate. Both types of filtering provide more control over internetwork traffic and better security.

Some bridges filter broadcast and multicast packets. This can help prevent traffic overloads called broadcast storms since these types of packets rarely go beyond the local LAN. In a broadcast storm, a broadcast message is repeatedly copied across bridges until the network screeches to a halt.

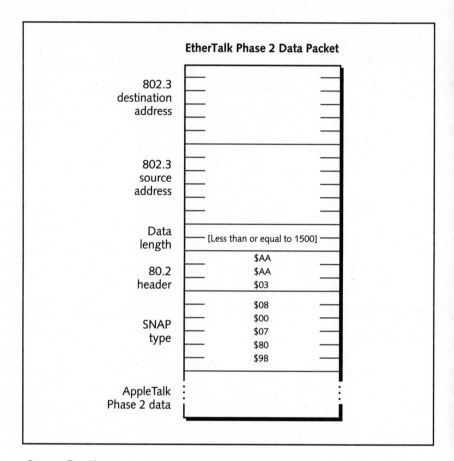

Figure 4-9 Schematic of an EtherTalk Data Packet

EtherTalk Phase 2 Data Packet

802.3 destination address

802.3 source address

Data length — [Less than or equal to 1500]

80.2 header
$AA
$AA
$03

SNAP type
$08
$00
$07
$80
$9B

AppleTalk Phase 2 data

Source Routing

Some token ring bridges, notably those from IBM, use a routing scheme called source routing to move packets between networks. The bridges we've talked about so far use transparent routing, which all Ethernet and StarLAN bridges and some token ring bridges use. With transparent routing, the packet does not know the route it will travel, nor do the bridges it passes over. Each bridge forwards a packet that is not local until it finally reaches its destination LAN.

With source routing, the packet itself contains its routing information. This information specifies the LANs and the bridge through which the packet will travel to get to its destination. The sending machine puts this information into the MAC layer packet header, the part of the packet which contains the source and destination addresses along with some other information about the packet.

In order for sending stations to know the route their packets will take, they must learn the layout of the entire network. This is done dynamically through a process called route discovery. During route discovery, packets are passed around the network. As they are passed from LAN to LAN, they are filled with information about the network. Each bridge a packet passes through puts three numbers into the packet: the number of the two LANs to which it is connected and its own bridge number. This information is then passed back to sending stations, which can then create a map of the network and appropriately route their packets.

A bridge at one end of the link puts packets destined for the other LAN out over the link.

Source routing is used primarily by IBM on token-ring LANs. Other vendors are beginning to use it, too. Source routing does impose some small amount of extra overhead on the network, but this is more than offset by the advantages of the routing scheme. Because the sending machine knows the route its packets will take, it can always choose the optimal path at the time of transmission, which is not possible with transparent routing. Also, source routing provides better management since the path of a packet is immediately accessible from the packet itself. Finally, source routing bridges can be faster than transparent bridges since they do not have to "look up" each packet to see if it might be bridged. The packet tells them immediately.

Remote vs. Local

So far, we have been discussing local bridges. Remote bridges connect two geographically separate LANs. Most of the time this is done with some type of communications link, like a telephone line, a public data network, a microwave or a T-1 (dedicated data) line. A bridge at one end of the link puts packets destined for the other LAN out over the link. A bridge at the other end of the link receives these and passes them to its local LAN. The process works in both directions.

Telecommunications links are not the only way to connect two LANs via a remote bridge. Broadband networks and fiber-optic links can also bridge two networks. For example, bridges might be used to pass traffic over a fiber-optic backbone between the buildings of a university or business campus or the branches of a bank. This is one of the most common uses of a bridge.

Either way, once bridges begin to connect LANs over a longer distance, reliability and fault tolerance become more important. Bridges at both ends must take precautions against data corruption over the remote link.

Spanning the Globe

An IEEE 802.1 algorithm or procedure called spanning tree makes it possible for a bridged network to include loops, a configuration that connects two ends of a bus topology, which are otherwise impossible with Ethernet. The spanning tree algorithm makes it possible to have parallel bridges so a backup bridge can take over in case the primary bridge fails. Without a backup bridge using spanning tree, a failed bridge causes the network to be partitioned until the broken bridge can be found and fixed.

According to the spanning tree algorithm, one bridge is designated the primary bridge. This bridge is the only bridge to pass traffic. If it fails, the traffic is automatically shunted to a parallel bridge. Nearly all bridges that support a backup bridge use the 802.1 spanning tree algorithm, although some have made nonstandard "improvements."

Spanning tree overcomes a major obstacle in bridging, but if the backup bridge is idle as it waits for a failure, that is costly. The solution is load balancing, dividing traffic evenly over the two remote parallel bridges. This provides much better performance, since not all traffic is going over one remote link. Since the spanning tree technology is still in place, loops are not an issue. If one bridge happens to fail, the other can carry all the traffic.

Bridges should have network management capabilities. These include providing information to the LAN manager on how much traffic is passing through, what type of traffic it is, how many errors occur, etc. With this information, the LAN manager can then configure and manage the network.

Routers

It's easy for newcomers to local area networks to be confused by bridges and routers, since they are so similar. A router is another little box that sits in the wiring closet near the hub and the bridge. Like the bridge, it has its own microprocessor and knows where the workstations are located. But a router is smarter than a bridge. It can look at more information in the packet before it passes the data from one side to another, and consequently has a higher price: from $5,000 to $20,000. The larger the network, the more likely it needs one of these devices.

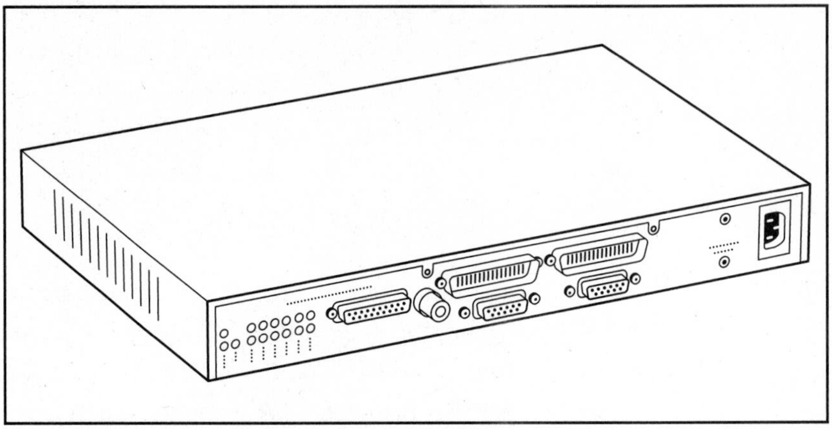

Figure 4-10 A Router

A router is like a bridge, except that it's more protocol dependent—it can only link two identical networks, such as two NetWare IPX LANs or a pair of VINES LANs. A router, like a bridge, moves data between networks only when specifically instructed by the network operating system.

While routers do as good a job of restricting local network traffic as bridges, they require more configuration to work properly. Routers also must exchange data among themselves periodically to keep an up-to-date snapshot of the network's topology. This additional network traffic usually doesn't affect network performance, but it can make a difference on larger networks with many routers.

In the past, bridges were more efficient than routers in processing and forwarding packets on a network, partly because they had less processing to do for each packet. However, with today's faster microprocessors, routers do not seriously affect network speeds.

Alternative Network Connections

Networks can be constructed out of almost anything that can transmit a signal. Whereas copper cabling is the most common means of carrying network signals, there's an increasing use of fiber-optic cables that use photons, or light signals, rather than electrons to carry the signals. Some networks also use wireless setups, such as infrared light or radio frequencies, to transmit signal over short distances. Large networks are often created using microwave or satellite links to connect geographically distant networks, such as when a large multinational corporation needs to link together all of its branch offices.

5 / LAN Applications

We've explained the basic ingredients of a local area network—the servers, workstations, connectors and network operating software. Now we need to approach the specific tasks you want to accomplish with this system.

Any software that helps you accomplish a specific task is called an application. Application software should be distinguished from system software, which is the software that the computer uses to accomplish tasks for application software. It should also be distinguished from network operating systems, which operate the various functions of the LAN. Applications have to do with the daily bread and butter of your business.

Application software includes:

- Word processing
- Database management
- Accounting
- Spreadsheets
- Desktop publishing
- Communications and electronic mail
- Enabling group action

Single-User vs. LAN Versions

There are important differences between application software that is designed to be used by one computer and application software designed for a LAN. Notably, single-user application programs are not written to keep others from using the same file at the same time. Single-user applications often can run on a network as long as they're run on a local workstation and any temporary or auxiliary files (like dictionaries) reside on the local hard drive. Of course, the data created can be stored on a file server, if desired.

On the other hand, applications designed for use on a LAN have to store temporary files on the user's local disk, or use different names for each temporary file created by a shared application, or be able to lock out changes in a file until the file's owner is finished, or warn other users when changes are being made and then send those changes to other users.

If you are using your LAN just to share printers or hard disk space, there may be no immediate need to change application software. Any LAN operating system allows single-user software to print to a networked printer, either directly or via a print server. However, technical constraints—and the license agreements you consented to by tearing the shrink wrap off your software applications—mean that only one person at a time should run single-user software, whether it is stored on a central server or at a local workstation. Single-user programs often maintain default settings and other information in files meant to be opened by only one user at a time. If a second user opens the same application on the server, a single-user application may either attempt to create a new settings file, destroying the first, or, even worse, simply crash the system.

In any case, there is a big difference between software that's merely usable on a LAN and software that actively uses the network. The special LAN version of a favorite program gives the user not just multiuser access to the applications, but also the ability to share databases, "boilerplate" text and other information. And all of this can be done whether users are in the same building or across the country, or whether communicating with someone at the same time or different times.

Software companies almost always give price breaks on LAN versions. They know that installing software on a LAN encourages new employees in a department to adopt the same product their colleagues are already using. It's cheaper to purchase a given program for the server and then pay a license fee based on the number of users than to buy a standalone version of the same application for each workstation.

Application Types

The term "application" actually has several meanings. In its most generic sense, the term applies to a task. For example, a widget maker needs to take orders over the phone and transmit the orders to a warehouse where the widgets are shipped to customers. The whole procedure might be called an order entry and inventory control application. In this sense, other applications include list management, accounting, design, marketing, sales, etc.—the tasks of any enterprise.

More specifically, the term application refers to the computer software used to get a particular job done. Thus, database management software like *dBASE IV, Paradox* and *Oracle* is called application software, as are other types of software like *WordPerfect, CrossTalk* and Lotus *1-2-3*. In this sense, application software is distinguished from system software, the software that makes the computer and LAN run. Think of the application software as running on top and taking advantage of the system software (and hardware).

The word application refers to specific programs written to perform a task.

Finally, the word application refers to specific programs written to perform a task. For example, many users have written applications in the dBASE language. These are customized programs (also applications) written by and for users, not by software vendors. This can get tricky, because some value-added retailers and system integrators also write such programs to sell. The difference is that they are not selling generic application software like Microsoft or Lotus Development but, like the users themselves, are creating customized programs using the software of software developers like Microsoft and Lotus Development.

In the world of LANs, there are three types of applications—LAN-ignorant, LAN-aware and LAN-intrinsic.

LAN-Ignorant Programs

LAN-ignorant applications are programs written for use on one computer by one user. However, these programs often run on the network; that is, they may be stored on a file server and used by LAN users at their workstations. Most of the time there are severe limitations on what these applications can do. Moreover, if two people try to use the program at the same time, many unintended things can happen. For example, the second user's settings or information files may overwrite those created when the first user launched the program, destroying whatever the first user did. Or, in some cases, the application may simply crash when the second user attempts to launch it.

LAN-Aware Programs

LAN-aware applications are a step above LAN-ignorant applications. Usually they are LAN-ignorant programs that have been modified to run on a network. These programs recognize that they will be used by several users at a time. They have concurrency control features like file and record locking to coordinate usage. For example, when a *Paradox* user begins to modify an address in a mailing list database, other users looking at the same mailing list at the same time are prevented from changing that address record. This is called record locking. When the change is complete, the change is displayed on the screen of every other user looking at the file. This is called automatic data or screen refresh.

File locking is a less sophisticated form of concurrency control. Instead of being kept out of a particular record, users are kept out of the entire file altogether while another user has it open. Word processing programs are the primary users of this type of concurrency control.

LAN-aware programs like *Paradox* make up the vast majority of programs written for networks. They represent a big improvement over LAN-ignorant applications and have gone a long way to spur the growth of networking. In fact, they are becoming so sophisticated that the distinction between LAN-aware and LAN-intrinsic is being blurred.

LAN-Intrinsic Programs

LAN-intrinsic applications actually share the processing power of several computers. Usually, though not always, this is done by dividing the application program into pieces. Depending on the number of computers actually participating in the calculation or sharing data, LAN-intrinsic applications are classified as either client-server or distributed processing applications.

In the client-server approach, only two computers participate in the application's task over the network. One computer, the client, talks to the user and prepares data to be sent to the server. The other computer, the server, does most of the data processing. In distributed processing, more than two computers communicate with each other and share the results of their computations over the network. We'll say more about distributed processing shortly.

A database server is the best example of a client-server application. Its principles can also be applied to other LAN-intrinsic applications. In a database server, there are also two parts to the application—the front end, or user interface, and the back end. The front end is responsible for formulating requests and displaying formatted data to the user. The back end is responsible for managing and searching data, concurrency control and security (see Figure 5-1). The front-end program takes care of making queries, writing reports, adding data to databases—all tasks it does with any other database management program. The difference is the way these tasks are handled.

For example, when a user asks the company database for all the employees who make more than $50,000, this request is transmitted to the database server (back end). The database server then searches for the employees making over $50,000. These records are then sent to the front end. This is different from the LAN-aware method.

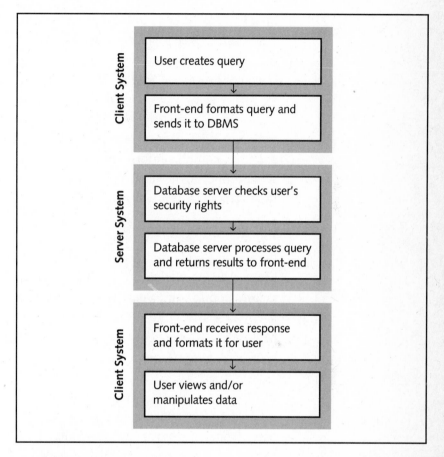

Figure 5-1
How Client-Server
Databases Operate

In the LAN-aware method, by contrast, there is only one program instead of two and it runs in the user's machine. When the request for high-paid employees is made, the program gets the whole database over the network from the file server, then searches it. The transfer creates much more network traffic than with the LAN-intrinsic method. At the same time, the database program has to ensure that other users cannot alter records and must send the changes immediately to all other users. This creates even more network traffic.

The database server (back end) eliminates the concurrency control traffic at the user's end and only the requested records are sent over the network instead of the whole database. The result is a more efficient, safer, better performing program and network. The reason this can be done is that two programs are working together to create one application—a true LAN-intrinsic application.

Database servers are also examples of distributed processing. If a number of database servers are connected together via the network and each contains information that the user needs, a query for data sent to one of the databases causes the other databases to include their data in the answer returned to the user.

For example, when planning your vacation, a travel agent may make both airline and hotel reservations at the same computer. When the agent asks for availability of a particular flight and seat, that information comes from a database that belongs to the airline. When the agent uses the same program to book you a room, the database responding to that request forwards the request to a different database belonging to the hotel chain.

Another example of distributed processing that's recently become interesting is rendering graphics images over a LAN. In this case, a user defines the image to be rendered on his or her workstation, then different computers on the network each calculate different parts of the image's rendering before sending the results back to the user's workstation.

Imagine that you want a new 3-D logo for your company's stock report. Your graphics designer sends you a sketch and, once it's approved, uses *RenderMan*, running on three networked computers, to create a realistic-looking final image. In the meantime, the initial layout of the stock report can be done using a page-layout program and the original sketch. When the rendered image is complete, it simply replaces the sketch in the page-layout file.

In the future, LAN-intrinsic programs will use their network links in more sophisticated methods. Rather than use a simple client-server architecture, future programs will take advantage of distributed processing, coupling together results and calculations from more than two computers on the network.

Word Processors

These days, nearly every major word processor program comes in a special LAN version. These products make it easy for users to use a LAN server to store documents that need to be accessed by others, and by offering a centralized dictionary, thesaurus, keyboard macros and style sheets, they help a department standardize formats for memos and correspondence.

"File compatibility and conversions will be a big issue in upgrading or changing software especially if it's something like word processing where people have a lot of files that need to get converted."
— LINDA MUSTHALER, MIS SPECIALIST, WEST COAST AEROSPACE

Of course, LAN word processors also offer each user the full resources of any shared printer, even when it's a laser printer that requires careful management of downloadable fonts. Some high-end programs incorporate document management facilities, letting users track revisions of a document via a "redlining" option that shows additions or deletions on screen.

WordPerfect includes all the features mentioned above. It can combine separate files into one master document with a single table of contents or index, and it imports a wide variety of graphics into *WordPerfect* documents. A particularly useful printing feature lets a user format text for a LAN printer and preview it on a local dot-matrix device with the closest approximate fonts.

Microsoft *Word*, the program that pioneered style sheets, now adds on-screen preview of both graphics and multiple column layouts. It has new document management features that let multiple users attach comments to a single document. When all reviewers are finished adding comments, an included macro merges all the annotations into a single file.

Databases

Ultimately, every business needs its very own database, whether it's an airline reservations system or package tracking system. Your business might be reserving tables at a restaurant or monitoring the parts at a lamp factory. But whatever it is, your company rises or falls on its ability to get the information you need, when you need it, where you need it and in the form you need it. LANs and databases provide that ability.

Simply put, a database is a collection of information organized for easy access and manipulation. An address book is a database. So is a recipe book, a catalog, a dictionary or a calendar. Usually, a database holds representative information, information that refers to something else, like food, people, clothing, words or days of the year—information we need to do our jobs and live our lives.

That information is only half the story, though. The other half is the road map explaining what the pieces of information mean and how they relate to each other. A phone number, for instance, needs to be connected to other information—a customer's name or history of orders. Creating a road map is an important component of building a database, and keeping that map up to date is how we keep it relevant to the real things it is describing.

So here's our working definition of a database: an organized collection of pieces of information, together with a road map that helps us understand what individual pieces of data mean and how they relate to one another.

Database Management Systems

The task of building the road map and then the necessary database into a computer can be formidable. Some databases are hundreds of megabytes in size. An entire branch of computer science has grown up around databases and any number of commercial database management systems (DBMSs) to provide database-related services. These services include database definition (building the road map), database conversion (importing data from a variety of sources into a database, or exporting it from the database into a variety of forms) and database management (keeping the data current, correct and safe from loss or harm).

The rise of the information sciences has had an interesting side effect—businesses and corporations now view their databases as resources with definite, mission-critical value, much like the people, money and fixed assets that they always recognized as vital to their operations.

Among the many things DBMSs do, controlling access to data, protecting data from accident or malicious intent, manipulating data and providing tools for the interpretation of data are the most important. A DBMS must provide fast, easy access to data, but it must also keep that data consistent and useful. The following features are important capabilities found in most DBMSes.

Database Design and Maintenance Tools

The initial design of a database requires using a data definition language (DDL). The database designer uses the DDL to describe the information content and structure of the database, defining the record types to be used and the ways in which the record types are related. For example, a database might contain text fields for employee first name, last name and address, and integer fields for the employee zip code and phone number. The designer would use the DDL to indicate that the employee's full name is the concatenation of two fields, the employee first name and the employee last name. Associated with the DDL is the data dictionary, which catalogs all relations between fields and all field attributes (number of characters or integer vs. text, for example). A user wanting to access data from a database first reviews the data dictionary to determine what information is stored where.

Data Administration and Control Mechanisms

These tools grant varying levels of privilege to users and restrict access accordingly. There are three principal levels of access: read access (look but don't touch), write access (change the contents of the database) and administrative (change the composition and distribution as well as the contents of the database). This last type of access allows a supervisor to change the structure and relationships of a database, something most users should not be able to do, since it can have grave effects on the integrity of data.

Data Entry Management Utilities

These software tools are used to enter data into the database. They range from simple prompt/response routines to elaborate screen forms that include all kinds of data-checking and relationship management information. Examples would be checking to make sure that the phone number has the correct number of digits or that the salary of an employee is more than a few dollars and less than a few million.

Report Design and Generation Utilities

These allow database programmers to design and name particular reports to be extracted from the contents of a database. For instance, a common report is a customer list, including names, addresses and telephone numbers. Once defined, a report can be generated at the push of a button, each time with the latest data available.

"People don't want to go to the library. They want information to come to them."

—RICHARD LUCIER, VICE CHANCELLOR, UNIVERSITY OF CALIFORNIA AT SAN FRANCISCO

Ad Hoc Query Facilities

These let database users question a database on the fly. For instance, you may want to ask how many people in your database are named Fred or how many live in Wisconsin. In a sense, query facilities permit users to obtain reports without having to design a regular form for delivering them.

Backup and Recovery Utilities

These software tools permit a database to be restored to a correct state when hardware, electrical or human failure causes its data to become suspect or corrupted. For instance, suppose a lightning strike near the office causes the computer and disk drive to lose power just as some new information is being added to the database. It is not clear if the changes were complete and recorded in the database. By rolling back the database to a state when everything was certain and then reentering the changes, users can be sure their changes are made. This process is called transaction rollback and recovery. It's a little like reversing time.

Together, this collection of capabilities constitutes a complete start-to-finish environment for setting up and managing databases.

New Developments

The biggest development in the LAN database arena is the PC database server. Every major database vendor has announced a PC database server or support for one. The first one came from Gupta Technologies several years ago. Before the advent of PC servers, minicomputer databases were used to implement the client-server architecture. Only recently, however, has client-server architecture attracted the interest of large software companies.

Database servers have several advantages over file-server-based DBMSes: they perform better, use less network bandwidth, save on workstation resources and are more reliable and secure in mission-critical applications. They also allow for other programs to use database information by programs other than database—for example, *Excel, 1-2-3* and *PageMaker.*

More exciting than database servers are distributed databases. Database servers form the basis for distributed databases, but they are not the same. Database servers have one server and many users. Distributed databases have many servers and many users. The differences are profound.

Distributed databases require the LAN to work transparently with data, regardless of where the data resides. A distributed database has two key functions. The first is the ability to do a relational join with two tables from two database servers. The second is the ability to write updates to two or more sites as part of one transaction.

A distributed database has two key functions. The first is the ability to combine data from two or more tables (a relational join, as it's called by database designers) where these tables reside on more than one database server. This combined data is then presented to the client. This transparency of where the data resides makes it easier for a user to request reports without knowing where the data is stored.

Second, not only must a distributed database be able to combine data from different servers for presentation to the client, but the database also has to be able to accept data from a client (a transaction) and use it to update the database. In particular, a distributed database must be able to take data from a single transaction and use it to update data that resides on two or more servers. Without this ability, each user would have to know how this data affects all the data in the database and would need to issue a transaction for each and every item of data that's affected.

"No one's throwing out the mainframe, but we do see people expanding to distributed computing and connecting to the mainframe. Users want tools for the new environment that give them the same functionality as mainframe systems management tools."
—KURT SEIBERT, COMPUTER ASSOCIATES INTERNATIONAL, INC.

Front Ends, SQL and Databases

The most popular way to acquire data from corporate databases on the network is to use a front end program that runs on a PC. This approach is becoming even more popular as more and more companies install database servers and distributed databases. A front end can help users in at least three cases:

- Wandering electronically throughout the network, pulling data from a variety of hosts
- Automating some reports so that they always print the latest data without having to rekey them
- Building full-blown applications for end users to access SQL databases.

At the moment, there is no "do-it-all" front-end application. Programs like Pioneer Software's *Q+E* and *ClearAccess* from ClearAccess Software are good for exploratory data searches, while tools like Microsoft's *Access* and Brio Technology's *DataPrism* are good for formatted reports. For creating applications for database access, there's Powersoft's *PowerBuilder* and Trinzic Corporation's *Forest and Trees*.

SQL, or Structured Query Language, has become the lingua franca of relational databases since its pioneering use by IBM in DB2. Now, all LAN-based relational and distributed databases offer some support for SQL. But SQL is not an easy language to use for constructing queries, especially if the user is only an occasional user of the database, like an upper-level manager using an Executive Information System. In such cases, it's much better to use SQL front ends to the databases. An SQL front end lets the user create or modify a query using either an English-like language or a graphical display. The front-end program then translates the query into one using SQL for transmittal to the database.

Accounting

For many companies, accounting software may be the reason for installing a LAN. Accounting information—accounts payable, accounts receivable, payroll, inventory—is a company's most important information. A network allows a company's books to be kept up to date by several data entry operators simultaneously, and means that completely up-to-date reports may be produced at any time.

Of the hundreds of accounting programs on the market, not all run on LANs. The Buyer's Guide (Chapter 10) describes many that do. We will discuss some exemplary ones here.

With its *AccPac* line, Computer Associates has a full range of network accounting software. *AccPac* BPI modules include Accounts Receivable and Payable, Payroll and Inventory Control. Running them on a LAN requires the *AccPac BPI Lan Pack*, which confers file and record locking plus password protection.

Data Pro's line of accounting programs is LAN-ready and significantly more complete than most. Modules include General Ledger, Accounts Payable with Checkwriting, Purchase Order Entry with On-Order Processing, Payroll (again with Checkwriting) and Job Costing with Time Billing. Point of Sale and Inventory Management modules support hardware add-ons, including cash drawers, bar-code readers and even speech synthesizers. The Data Pro modules, which have a consistent user interface, can either stand alone or operate as part of an integrated system.

Particularly useful for tailoring accounting software to a business is the SBT *Database Accounting Library*. SBT offers a particularly wide range of modules, including Professional Time and Billing, Project Accounting, Purchasing and many others written in *dBASE* source code. Users can modify the program and run them using any *dBASE* interpreter.

Spreadsheets

Spreadsheets are fundamentally personal productivity tools, so their LAN versions are not dramatically different from the single-user ones. But network versions of spreadsheet programs offer a saving in cost and workstation disk space, and they are more convenient to load. Most important, they always prevent multiple users from changing the same worksheet concurrently by mistake.

Underlining the growing importance of LANs, all current versions of Lotus *1-2-3* include network support as a standard feature. Lotus *1-2-3* Release 3.x, which allows loading multiple spreadsheets into as much as 16MB of memory (on 80286 or 80386 PCs), features file locking and support for either DOS or OS/2-compatible LANs. It comes in a single-user edition, but a server edition lowers the price of adding workstations.

LAN versions always prevent multiple users from changing the same worksheet concurrently.

Lotus *1-2-3* Release 2.x, which comes with the Allways print formatting program built in and has been tailored to the existing base of DOS networks and 8088 PCs, comes in a server edition. The workstation edition (consisting of a software license and documentation only) is relatively inexpensive.

Microsoft *Excel* also runs across LANs, printing to network devices via its Windows user interface. With small fields such as those created by *Excel*, it's particularly useful to be able to offload them to a LAN server; because of differing workstation configurations, though, it's best to keep Windows itself on local disk drives. Only a single person may have read/write access to a worksheet at any one time, but *Excel* optionally lets others look at it without making changes. The very similar Macintosh version can trade worksheets with PC *Excel*. It now stores spreadsheets up to 8MB in size on Macs that have the RAM.

Desktop Publishing

Though most desktop publishing programs can be installed on LAN servers and run from one workstation at a time, it's still rare to find one that handles simultaneous multiuser access to files. With its Network Edition, however, *Ventura Publisher* can make that claim. *Quark XPress* also allows Mac and Windows users to share desktop publishing files over a network.

The file server software allows all workstations to share a printer, chapter layouts and source text files. A special alert notifies a user when a file within a chapter has been modified by another user, and multiple workstations can share the same read-only style sheets. *Ventura* does have rather stringent hardware requirements. Each workstation must have a full 640KB of RAM, plus at least 256KB of expanded memory.

Integrated Software

Integrated software packages combine word processing, database management and spreadsheet applications in one product. The advantages of integrated software include its consistent commands and menus and the easy transfer of information from one module to another. Integrated software packages can, however, benefit from networking in the same way as their standalone counterparts.

Lotus' *Symphony* includes a locking utility that supports worksheet sharing over the LAN, and it has graphics built in. *Open Access II Plus* includes a multifile database, spreadsheet, word processor and desktop utilities.

Informix Software takes a modular approach with its *Smart Software System*. This LAN integrated software, including a word processor and spellchecker, spreadsheet and database manager, may be purchased as separate modules or all at once. Adding workstations is easy; just purchase access software for each new machine.

Among the very cheapest LAN applications on the market is Microsoft's *Works*, a simple integrated package whose spreadsheet reads and writes Lotus *1-2-3* files. The Macintosh version of *Works* runs over networks compatible with Apple's AppleTalk Filing Protocol (AFP), letting several users access files in read-only mode.

Electronic Mail

An array of excellent e-mail products is now available to LAN users, offering not only advanced messaging features but powerful internetworking and gateway links to other mail systems. But selecting the appropriate e-mail package isn't a straightforward task. While many e-mail products share a common set of necessary features, there are enough differences in how they implement various features and support different computing platforms that there is no one market leader.

When shopping for e-mail, there are at least four features to look for on the client or user side and three main features to look for on the server or administration end. For the user, the main features are a simple yet functional interface, personal address lists, provisions for enclosing files and remote access to the server. Desirable server-side features are directory synchronization, gateways to other mail systems and server management tools. Security is also an important issue, to user and administrator alike.

User Issues

E-mail should be easy to use. If you had to make your own paper, get a special government permit to affix a stamp to the envelope and run down to a neighborhood office to find out someone's address code before mailing, you probably wouldn't use the postal system very much. E-mail's the same way; everything has to be at the user's fingertips.

Although there is no standard user interface to e-mail, all products offer a basic set of features that the user can easily access. Basically, users should be able to compose a text message, select an address and send the message with a minimum of fuss. They should also be able to be notified of incoming mail and read their mail easily. To utilize e-mail effectively, respect the common aversion to too many buttons or menus and stick with a simple interface.

"Administration is a real issue. Without the right tools, a mail system can eat your lunch."

—DURWIN SHARP, EXXON

More than simple access to the e-mail program (via a TSR on a DOS computer or a desk accessory on a Mac), users need the underlying resources of the e-mail system to be readily available: an address book containing people's e-mail addresses and a means of composing the mail message. Fortunately, every e-mail vendor has recognized that displaying the user directory for the entire company is not an efficient way to show the user the address he or she wants. Users can search the entire company directory if they want (for an infrequent correspondent, for example), but it's much easier to use a personal address book, which contains frequently used addresses. Some e-mail programs let users maintain more than one personal address book.

These addresses are not necessarily restricted to individuals, either. One option adding to the usefulness of e-mail is the group address. Group addresses assign a name to a group of individual addresses, say, all the people in the accounting department. Then, when someone uses the group address "Accounting" for sending e-mail, a copy of the message is sent to everyone in the accounting department with one keystroke.

Most messages on e-mail are simple: planning schedules, arranging a meeting or forwarding a phone message. But users can also use e-mail to send files as enclosures to messages. At a minimum, most e-mail products let users attach a single file as an enclosure. Some allow them to attach an unlimited number of files, but let the system administrator place a limit on the total size of the enclosures.

Over the past few years, a revolution has been taking place in personal computers. Users are coming to rely increasingly on mobile computing, using notebooks and laptops in the field for a broad variety of tasks that used to be done only at their desks. And these users want to keep in touch with the home office, so they need to be able to use their e-mail while they're on the road. That means they need remote access to their e-mail servers. And, if they can do so with the same interface as the one they use at their desktop computers, so much the better.

Administrator Issues

Within a single-server environment, the task of maintaining an e-mail system is somewhat simplified. The common chores are adding accounts to the mail directory and purging the system of old mail. Setting up rules within the mail server to automatically delete any mail older than 30 days, or to archive all messages older than that, can be very helpful for providing faster server response as well as freeing up disk space.

Local area network administrators working within a multiple-server environment should shop for an e-mail system that supports directory synchronization. Since each server can maintain its own list of users, the basic idea is to provide a mechanism for the servers to share their user lists (directories) so that mail can be exchanged between the servers. Most systems allow this exchange of directories to take place on a peer-to-peer basis (all servers share equally), but *cc:Mail* also provides an option to create a hierarchy of servers.

Each e-mail system has its own format for user directories, so it's difficult, if not impossible, to support e-mail products from different vendors on the same LAN. Companies such as Soft*Switch offer mainframe-based and minicomputer-based products that maintain a master directory that other e-mail products access via a gateway. On the horizon as a solution to this directory mess is the X.500 standard. As vendors provide X.500 directory support within their e-mail products, integrating directories from different products will become much easier.

> ### The Haves and the Have Nots
> Since a well-designed network can span the country and it's just as easy to send an e-mail message across the office as around the world, e-mail users may find themselves deluged with messages that they must sift through. And e-mail, unless implemented consistently throughout a firm, tends to stratify a company into the group on the net and the group that isn't.
>
> —R. Needleman, InfoWorld

While small LANs are usually self-sufficient, many companies want to link together their LANs, especially if they're located in different cities. Others might also want to share e-mail with clients using other mail systems. In either case, they probably need a gateway or two. These gateways are usually installed either on one of the servers or on a dedicated PC. They assume the responsibility of translating addresses and message contents between e-mail formats so that different systems can communicate.

When it comes to handling text-only messages, gateways do not pose too many problems. The problems arise when users include file enclosures or use multimedia mail. Since different e-mail systems format their messages differently from each other, a gateway may not be able to translate all items accompanying one message to comparable items for a differently formatted message. Some systems support only text, so enclosures including sound or animation are lost when translated by the gateway.

Security Issues

The security of the e-mail system is an important concern, especially if you're conducting company business with it. At a minimum, mail administrators should ensure that users are assigned passwords and that they frequently change passwords. The next step, encrypting message contents, hasn't been implemented by many vendors, but should start showing up in quite a few mail packages this year as vendors settle on encryption standards.

Cross-Platform Issues

All major mail packages can send and receive text messages between different platforms, particularly DOS and Macintosh. But if messages include images or sound, translation isn't always possible, although products like *cc:Mail* include translators to assist in the process.

The real problem for a combined Mac-DOS LAN is file enclosures. Much of this is due to the dual-fork nature of Macintosh files. The Mac stores file information in two different file parts, the data fork and the resource fork. But DOS systems usually only know how to deal with the part called the data fork. Thus, to exchange files via e-mail between Mac and DOS computers, Mac users should take care to use third-party utilities (such as those from Apple and DataViz) to save their files in a DOS-compatible mode before mailing.

The major e-mail packages are Lotus' *cc:Mail*, Microsoft's *Mail*, *WordPerfect Office*, *Da Vinci eMail* and CE Software's *QuickMail*, all of which offer servers and clients for both DOS and Macintosh computers. Other interesting programs that offer new features for handling e-mail, such as automated responses to messages and filing of incoming messages, include Reach's *MailMAN* and Beyond's *BeyondMail*.

Groupware

The term "groupware" covers a wide range of new software products that aren't easily classified. What all have in common is taking isolated PC users and bringing them into a group. Thanks to these programs, which are usually priced on a per-server basis, members of a group need not be in the same place—or time—in order to work together.

The most common types of groupware applications are group schedulers, editing programs, workflow and document management systems, meeting facilitation and communications management systems.

Lotus Development Corporation's *Notes* is the leading workgroup communications program. Three main features that *Notes* rests on are advanced message security, an easy-to-use high-performance database and database replication. *Notes* also uses an advanced data-security technique from RSA Data Security Inc. to send messages marked with digital signatures, which are encoded strings of digits particular to the user, like an exclusive password.

Notes allows users to design templates for entering and viewing data, which can be shared across multiple databases. The templates can include macros written with a language similar to that used in Lotus *1-2-3*. Data can also be entered into, or selected from, the *Notes* database via e-mail. Now version 3.0 makes possible a centralized approach to shared information, since *Notes* 3.0 includes a centralized data dictionary, allowing users to ensure uniformity of data definitions and templates across servers and workgroups. For those interested in tracking and sharing images, Lotus has a *Notes* add-on, *Lotus Notes:Document Imaging (LN:DI)*, which handles scanned images.

Windows for Workgroups, as Microsoft's first foray into groupware, takes a different approach by providing users with tools for building their own groupware system. *Windows for Workgroups* includes e-mail, *Schedule+* (for scheduling meetings and such), a network clipbook for sharing data between users and NetDDE as a foundation for other communicating between networked applications.

Conetics Systems' *Higgins* handles office administration, allowing users to coordinate their schedules. It includes desktop accessories such as note pads, calculators, expense reports, to-do lists, tickler files and phone directories. *Higgins Exchange* can link LAN e-mail to external e-mail services such as CompuServe.

Office Works, a program from Data Access, offers similar functions and adds built-in database software that allows users to share name-and-address files and other lists. Chronos Software's *Enterprise* integrates people, project and time management. When the program is started, it displays a calendar, but users can switch to linked views of the projects they are working on or people they work with. Finally, *The Coordinator*, an elaborate electronic mail system, includes a system of management tools that track work commitments. It forces workgroup members to be explicit about what they promise to do and nags them to meet deadlines.

WordPerfect Office, as its name implies, is ideal for those already using *WordPerfect* for word processing. This product features a shell that can simplify LAN operation, allowing a user to switch applications and move text between them with a clipboard. *WordPerfect*

"All these tools have to do with information pull—how users weed through all the electronic information they receive to reach the right information in the right context, in the right format, and in realtime."

— LAURE ROWAN,
NETWORK
MANAGER, FORTUNE
100 FIRM

Office also has macros, electronic mail and a scheduler that automatically finds open times when department meetings can be scheduled. Its simple flat-file database module, Notebook, saves mail or telephone lists as *WordPerfect* merge files.

Other groupware products include *ActionTracker Plus*, *Shoebox*, *Telephone Note Taker Plus*, *TimeTalk*, *Schedule+*, *Meeting Maker*, *WorkMan* and IBM's *Person to Person/2*.

PART TWO

6 / Internetworking

Local area networks don't have to be all that local. The same LAN that links together employees in your company's accounting department can also be used to network the workers in human resources and data processing. In fact, LANs can be interconnected to connect people located in offices around the world. In practical terms, a LAN's boundaries can be as limitless as its users' needs and financial resources.

Internetworks

The easiest way to extend a LAN's scope is to connect the system to another nearby LAN. The second LAN can be located in the department next door or on the next floor. Integrating two or more LANs into a single large network creates a system known as an internetwork or internet. If those LANs are in two different cities or countries, the result is known as a wide area network, or WAN.

All WANs are internetworks, but not all internetworks are WANs. The internetwork consisting of a series of linked LANs in an office building is not a WAN, for instance.

Internetworks are usually created when an organization needs to provide all users with full access to its network resources. With an internetwork, Mary on the fifth floor and Joe on the sixth floor can each access applications, print documents, exchange electronic mail, swap files and work together as if they were working next to each other. If the internetwork happens to be intercontinental in scope, Pierre in Paris, Martina in Moscow, Mary on the fifth floor and Joe on the sixth floor can all be equal partners on the network. Figure 6-1 shows a typical nationwide internetwork.

Figure 6-1
A Typical Nationwide
Internetwork

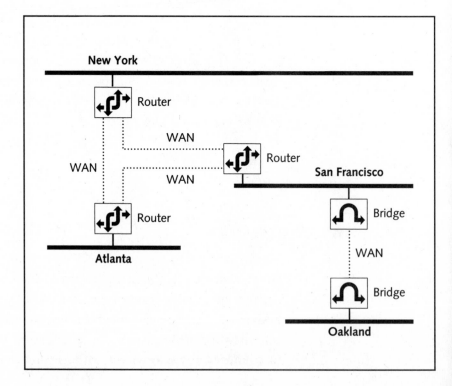

Benefits

The reasons for creating a WAN or internetwork are generally the same as for installing a LAN:

- Connectivity—To allow users to exchange files, e-mail and other information
- Peripheral access—Not as important as in a LAN, but handy when a remote user needs to output a lengthy document on a printer miles away, for example
- Database access—To give users in disparate locations easy access to critical information
- Value-added services—Electronic mail, "groupware" calendaring/scheduling applications and similar office automation services can promote cohesion and boost productivity between workers across the entire organization.

As with a LAN, many of the benefits of a WAN or internetwork are obvious while others are more subtle. In addition to the benefits cited above, veteran network managers note that new users should be aware of several annoying, critical drawbacks.

Drawbacks

The major drawbacks of WANs and internetworks, as with so much of computing, revolve around incompatibility—incompatible hardware platforms, network structures and network operating systems.

For example, what if network A is Ethernet-based while network B is built around token-ring technology? Both products have different throughputs, and dysfunctions can result when a bridge tries to force information from a high-speed Ethernet LAN into a slower token ring network, or vice versa. The answer is to find a bridge or gateway and related support products that can handle the speed difference and other incompatibilities between the technologies.

For another example, what if the users on network A are taking advantage of Novell's NetWare while network B is based on Microsoft LAN Manager? The best solution is to standardize on one NOS or the other.

Hardware platform differences aren't as problematic as they were in the past. Novell NetWare 3.11, for example, provides complete client support for all of the major desktop computer operating systems, including DOS, OS/2, Unix and Macintosh.

A popular and cost-effective technique for low-traffic networks is to use voice-grade telephone lines with standard asynchronous modems.

When linking various types of LANs, it's important to remember the difference between bridges, routers and gateways. Here are the definitions:

Bridges link separate LANs with different hardware and different protocols. They can also separate LANs so that if one system in city A has a problem, the LANs in city B won't be affected. It's important to acquire a bridge that meets the precise requirements of the situation (e.g., connecting an Ethernet LAN to a token-ring LAN).

Routers connect LANs with the same protocols but different hardware. Again, it's important to use the right type.

Gateways link LANs with different protocols by translating between them. A bridge does no translation.

Because of the different products involved, as well as the specific needs of the operator, each WAN or internetwork is really a custom job. The issue of compatibility should be addressed early in the planning stages of any WAN or internetworking project.

Moving Data via Voice-Grade Lines

When establishing a WAN or internetwork, the owner can choose from several ways of moving data between the different LAN sites. A popular and cost-effective technique for low-traffic networks is to use voice-grade telephone lines with standard asynchronous modems. The drawback to this approach is the relatively slow data transfer speeds of even today's most advanced asynchronous modems.

Buying a modem, once a relatively easy task, has grown more complicated over the years. In the past, nearly all modems operated at rates of 1,200 or 2,400 bits per second, so you simply shopped around and found the most durable unit at the best price.

But new and sophisticated data transfer, error protection and data compression standards are making modem shopping complicated. Terms like V.22, V.25bis and MNP Level 5 are heralded as key selling points by modem manufacturers, but make little sense to the average computer manager who's simply looking to ship data from one location to another quickly and cheaply. Here are explanations of the terms that you're most likely to see in manufacturers' literature:

- V.22, V.22bis—These standards reflect "stock," general-purpose modems capable of synchronous/asynchronous full-duplex data transmissions over standard phone lines. V.22 supports a 1,200 bps data rate; V.22bis supports 1,200 and 2,400 bps rates.

- V.25, V.25bis—Modems that support these standards provide automatic calling and answering circuitry for use on standard phone lines. V.25 defines a dial-up parallel interface, V.25bis a serial interface.

- V.32—This is the standard for general-purpose synchronous/asynchronous 9,600 bps modems (with automatic fallback to 4,800 bps if conditions dictate). V.32-compatible modems can operate on standard phone lines and are very useful for sending large volumes of data. They are quickly becoming the most popular modem type.

- V.32bis—These modems take full advantage of standard telephone lines to move information at speeds of up to 14,400 bps. Here's how it works: two V.32bis-compatible modems are linked together. As the units communicate, they automatically and continuously assess the quality of the phone line and jointly raise and lower their operating speeds to meet existing conditions. The only major limitation to the technology is that both modems must be V.32bis-compatible. V.32bis technology represents the most efficient way to move data over a standard phone line today.

- V.33—This standard supports synchronous, full-duplex operation over four-wire leased lines at 14,400 or 12,000 bps data rates. V.33-compatible modems are mostly used in collaboration with big machines such as mainframes and supercomputers. It's not a standard most PC managers have to worry about.

- V.13—This is another relatively obscure standard that most PC managers don't have to concern themselves with. V.32 and V.33-compatible modems use V.13 to provide simulated half-duplex control.

- MNP Levels 1-4—The MNP (Microcom Networking Protocol) was developed and patented by Microcom Inc., although the technology is now offered by other modem makers as well. An MNP modem, when connected to another MNP modem, can deliver asynchronous, error-free data over ordinary phone lines.

- MNP Level 5—This version adds a data compression algorithm to the error-correction capabilities of MNP Levels 1-4. It compresses data by a factor of two-to-one, allowing information to be sent much faster than with an equivalent modem lacking the protocol. A pair of MNP Level 5 modems rated at 9,600 bps can exchange data at an effective rate of 19,200 bps.

- V.42, V.42bis—These are error-correction and data compression protocols, respectively. Two V.42-compatible modems work together via a technology called link access protocol to ensure fault-free data transmission. A V.42-type modem connected to an MNP-compatible modem safeguards data with MNP. V.42bis roughly corresponds to MNP Level 5, although V.42bis can usually generate a four-to-one data compression ratio (depending on the type of file being transferred).

Various software products are available to connect LANs to modems. These packages range from simple "remote control" programs to sophisticated LAN linking packages. Most NOSes also provide some type of modem support, either built directly into the product or available as an option.

Leased Lines and Public Data Networks

For high-volume networks, a leased dedicated data line is a better choice than a voice-grade phone link. Commonly called T-1, a dedicated data line offers high-speed performance at a somewhat loftier cost. The technology can be leased from the local phone company at a price beginning at around $1,500 per month.

Network operators for whom a leased line is out of budget range may instead consider the use of a public data network. These systems use a protocol called X.25 established by the Consultative

Committee for International Telephone and Telegraph (CCITT), a United Nations organization that sets worldwide communications standards. X.25 services are offered to users by companies including Telenet and Tymnet.

Unlike leased-line customers, X.25 service users don't have to pay a big upfront charge—the companies generally charge a small subscription fee and then charge for the amount of time actually used. There are two ways of connecting to an X.25 service: with a gateway that's compatible with the network or via a modem.

To summarize:

- Voice-grade line with modem is low-cost for low-traffic networks, high-cost for medium and high-traffic networks.
- Leased dedicated data line is high-cost for low- and medium-traffic networks, low-cost for high-traffic networks.
- X.25 service is low-cost for low- and medium-traffic networks, high-cost for high-traffic networks.

To determine which approach best suits your wide area network and internetwork needs, you will have to examine the price of each service you will use and the traffic you expect to send between your LANs.

New Technologies

Several new communications technologies promise to reduce the cost of moving data between LANs. While none of these products are yet in widespread use, WANs can be built ready to take advantage of these breakthroughs as they become available.

ISDN

The most intriguing of these technologies is called Integrated Services Digital Network (ISDN). For more than a decade, trade journals, magazine advertisements, conferences and trade shows have been touting the technology's potential. But despite the publicity, ISDN has yet to make a meaningful impact in the WAN/internetwork field.

The technology is designed to integrate voice, data and other forms of electronic communications through a common interface over ordinary phone lines.

ISDN was outlined in the late 1970s by the CCITT. The technology is designed to integrate voice, data and other forms of electronic communications through a common interface over ordinary phone lines. Everything sent through ISDN is digitally encoded, even voice communications. Most appealing to internetwork users is ISDN's capability to support two 64,000 bps data streams and another signaling stream running at 16,000 bps. These higher-speed transmissions can be more useful for dial-up connections than regular high-speed modems.

The promised benefits of ISDN are increased efficiency and improved communications management. With ISDN, users can take advantage of a high-speed, reliable, globally available, competitively priced data transmission service. Eventually, ISDN's advocates see the technology reaching large and small businesses and even, by the turn of the century, home telephone users.

After years of promises and delays, the fundamental hardware necessary for ISDN is finally falling into place. AT&T, Sprint and other carriers announced ISDN service availability a couple of years ago. AT&T and other vendors have also unveiled ISDN switches for use in central telephone company switching offices. A national network that will support ISDN calls is now in the works and should become fully functional by the end of the decade.

Fiber-Optic Links

While fiber-optic technology is making some inroads in LAN cabling, its greatest potential may lie in internetworks. In the next century, when local phone companies and long-distance carriers complete the changeover to fiber optics, it will become possible to move data between sites at speeds of up to 100 million bits per second. At that rate, the entire contents of the *Encyclopaedia Britannica* could be moved between LANs in less than one second.

There are other advantages as well. Since fiber-optic systems transmit data as a series of light pulses, the technology is impervious to electrical noise and interference. As a result, error rates caused by cabling are dramatically lower with fiber optics than conventional cabling technology, improving throughput even more.

When it becomes generally available, fiber-optic technology will do much to solve the myriad problems facing LAN operators who need to move data from one location to another quickly and inexpensively.

Internetworking Pitfalls

Linking together departmental networks can boost productivity and trim costs, but before plunging ahead with networking plans, be sure to fully consider the problems that can quickly short-circuit them.

For example, after linking together two or more LANs into a WAN, the users may need better and more powerful software applications. The programs that satisfied the needs of, say, a dozen users may not be up to the rigors of serving 50 or more users with different needs and expectations.

Consider also the need for closer and more demanding network management. The tools and procedures that worked fine on a small LAN may fall flat on a larger WAN. Veteran WAN administrators know that problems only multiply as a network grows in size and scope. Security problems expand with a WAN as well. With more workstations and users online, the opportunities for data theft, virus introductions and other administrative headaches grow accordingly.

And don't forget the potential for turf wars. Individual department managers tend to feel very protective of their own LANs. The introduction of a WAN, with new users and resources, can cause uneasiness among managers who feel a loss of control over their LAN. Handling these problems may require a wide range of diplomatic skills.

In sum, don't expect to create a seamless network infrastructure overnight. The road to the perfect WAN or internetwork will take knowledge, skill and perseverance.

7 / LAN Administration

Successful LAN administrators do more than run networks. They ensure that the network is running as well as possible, and they plan the course of future expansion. Moreover, they communicate effectively with their users and the organization at large, teaching people about the network and learning how the network can better serve its users.

They must often act as evangelists to win the support of their superiors and gain the respect and resources needed to perform the many tasks involved in administering a LAN. Finally, they protect the network from equipment breakdowns, loss of data, human malfeasance and any other loss of capability that might hinder crucial network functions. (This last task is covered in Chapter 8, LAN Security.) To succeed in their jobs, effective LAN administrators must know their company's business, be well organized, have excellent communication skills, teach users effectively and possess an inspiring enthusiasm for LANs and what LANs can do.

But before a LAN administrator can begin to do that job, the whole organization must decide what it wants from a network, assess its support needs and allocate resources accordingly. This chapter presents the basic responsibilities of a LAN administrator and discusses the skills that will help accomplish those tasks. It also demonstrates how much of a LAN administrator's success depends on the support of the entire organization. Finally, it discusses the software tools available to help administrators do their job.

The Seven Basic Tasks

Although every LAN administrator faces tasks unique to his or her particular job, all administrators must address certain basic needs. LAN administrators from companies with fewer than ten people to megacorporations like Bank of America and Pacific Bell all must deal with the same seven fundamental responsibilities. Some of these are discussed in greater detail later in this chapter.

One: Running the Network

LAN administrators are responsible for developing a systematic, prevention-oriented approach to routine network maintenance tasks. This includes most of the daily tasks involved in sustaining the networks: adding users, arranging who has access to what data, monitoring traffic, making backups, accounting, cleaning up the file server hard disk, problem solving and similar tasks.

While these functions are crucial, they should not take up most of the administrator's time. Planning for the future, testing new technology, preparing documentation, training users and other general management issues are just as important. Administrators save time by limiting support to only a few chosen applications and not letting users install their own software at will. They establish company standards for each type of software, so there is an "official choice" for word processing, spreadsheet and database software. Diagnostic utilities can help them spot problems before they become serious. Making the network as easy to use as possible and transparent to end users can also dramatically reduce the amount of time spent on basic support.

Two: Getting the Best Performance

Administrators must get the most out of the software and hardware they have. They check for performance bottlenecks, make sure that hardware and software are keeping up with demand, and determine patterns of use and modify the network configuration accordingly.

The bulk of performance management should concentrate on the system components where most application activity takes place. That may be a particular database server or perhaps a modem server if many users are frequently on the road.

For example, if the publications group is slowing down the network print queue by printing long documents from a desktop publishing program, a print server dedicated to this group could speed up printing for the rest of the organization. Or if the marketing group is filling up the file server with huge graphic files, the administrator can show them how to compress graphics before storing them.

Three: Expanding Capabilities

Administrators find creative ways the network can make the office more productive, adding new software and hardware to expand the capabilities and keep up with demand. They stay in tune with the basic direction of the organization and use the network to help meet its goals.

For example, the administrator may see that salespeople are wasting time printing out documents to be sent by fax. After installing a fax card in the server, or setting up a dedicated fax server, they can do a job in only 10 seconds that used to take 5 minutes.

Four: Teaching Users

Teach users before they get into trouble.

Administrators help users increase their knowledge so they don't have to spend all their time solving users' problems. The more users understand, the easier the administrator's job will be, so administrators should take the lead in this area and teach users *before* they get into trouble. They should keep up with the industry to be good teachers.

Good LAN administrators develop special documentation for their own network. They document every procedure that's specific to the network and the applications it uses. For example, they write down the backup procedure so that backups will be performed correctly when the administrator cannot be there. This documentation is good not only for users but also for training backup administrators.

Five: Learning From Users

Successful administrators develop structured ways for users to offer suggestions and comments about the network. The best ideas for increasing productivity often come from users. Interested users from all departments should be encouraged to participate in the network steering committee, where they can offer feedback on current systems and recommend new ones.

Learning from users involves studying how people do their jobs and finding ways to help them with the LAN. Administrators learn as much as they can about all operations from everyone, not just network users. This helps them expand the network into new areas.

They need to be accessible, understanding and responsive. They might spend a day in the accounting department and see if the accounting system is slowing down work there. They may ask the office manager why he still circulates memos on paper and never uses electronic mail, or ask someone in sales why she prefers her own word processing program to the company standard product.

Six: Budgeting and Reporting

LAN administrators develop ways to quantify productivity and then publish their results to the rest of the organization. They carefully record all costs and use these records to write accurate budgets. Creating new forms and special reports on productivity, cost and other issues can visibly define their product—a healthy LAN—to the rest of the organization.

"Documentation improves network integrity because problems get researched and resolved faster."
— NETWORK MANAGER, FORTUNE 100 FIRM

Reports should show which departments and which users require the most support time. They should show what types of problems take the most time to solve and how much they are costing the organization. They should assign to different departments various network costs according to how much they use network resources.

These reports tell top management and the rest of the organization what the LAN administrator is going to do, how it will be done and what's been accomplished. Otherwise, the executives may not appreciate the administrator's importance until something breaks.

Seven: Protecting the Network

This task includes estimating the cost of failure and loss of equipment and data and taking precautions in accordance with the degree of risk. Administrators develop fail-safe security systems and backup routines to prepare for acts of God or malice. They make sure to carefully grant access rights to important data so that novice users can't accidentally damage or delete it. They anticipate acts of vandalism, not only to equipment but also to data. They make sure that crucial network equipment is physically protected (preferably in a locked room) and that only authorized users have access to important data, and they keep up-to-date backups in safe, off-site storage. They devise disaster plans that anticipate the type of total loss that might result from a fire, hurricane, tornado, earthquake or other calamity and forecast how long and how much it would cost to get crucial functions working again. They should also research the temporary off-site options offered by disaster recovery specialists. This crucial basic task is covered in more detail in Chapter 8, LAN Security.

Maximizing Software and Hardware Performance

One of the simplest ways for a LAN administrator to improve a network is to replace old and slow components with newer devices that work faster or better. As networks grow, the LAN administrator must eventually replace components that are limiting the network's performance. Here are the key components they should pay continuing attention to.

Application and System Software

Software products are in a constant state of flux, with both completely new software packages and updated versions of older products arriving on a regular basis. Whether it's an application, like a word processor or a spreadsheet, or a system software product, like a network operating system, it nearly always pays to use the latest version. Product developers are always working to add new features and boost the overall performance of their products. The relatively small cost of upgrading current software is almost always more than repaid over the long run.

Savvy administrators also regularly read trade publications, attend trade shows and talk to colleagues to learn about the latest products. For example, while the reliable old ABC database may have served network users well for the past five years, it's possible that the brand-new DEF product may perform even better. Trade contacts can also alert administrators to new products and upgrades that are plagued with problems.

Inadequate Hardware

The latest software, particularly products using a graphic user interface, requires faster, more powerful computers with a lot of memory.

Network users regularly run out of storage space. Generally speaking, it's less expensive to buy a slightly larger hard disk than to run out of room earlier than anticipated. Disk space can also be conserved by storing or archiving older, rarely used data on tape.

As organizations keep more and more data on larger hard disks, the previous generation of tape backup systems becomes sorely inadequate. Some systems require frequent tape swapping—and the chances for a data error increase exponentially with every new tape. Administrators sometimes complain of hours wasted every week on tape backups.

Slow printers cause one of the most noticeable and irritating network delays. An impatient crowd of users waiting for their urgently needed documents to come out of the printer often means trouble for the LAN administrator.

Adding Enhanced Components

In general, upgrading to higher-performance hardware or software doesn't require any advanced modeling or simulation. Since no entirely new function is being added to the network, there are few variables. As long as the new device or software works correctly, it should usually improve network performance.

LAN administrators should thoroughly test any new equipment or software before adding it to the network. A new system may solve a few old problems while introducing a whole series of new ones that can reflect poorly on the administrator.

Administrators need to develop realtime metrics to measure how well services are being delivered to the user.

In evaluating new components for a network, there are two main approaches: benchmark testing and on-the-job testing. Benchmark testing involves comparing performance statistics, such as processor speed and hard disk access time. Most manufacturers provide a wealth of these statistics, but there are also programs (usually designed for testing computers) that can verify these numbers and provide many other performance statistics. Many computer publications also publish the benchmarks of various products.

Since each network is different and every user has unique priorities, on-the-job testing means actually using the new device and systematically tracking its performance. For testing a computer, this might mean timing how long it takes to recalculate a spreadsheet or to query a database. Administrators need to develop realtime metrics to measure how well services are being delivered to the user. For example, they might measure how often modem servers are available during working hours, or time a database's response to standard queries.

When making any type of improvement to a LAN, an administrator should keep the following points in mind:

- **Upgrade only for improvement.** Many software and hardware products are continually upgraded. Make sure that the new features offered are really needed before going through any complex upgrade process. Generally, it makes more sense to stick to major new version upgrades (e.g., Version 1.0 to Version 2.0) rather than maintenance upgrades (e.g., Version 2.0 to Version 2.1), unless the minor upgrade contains an important new feature or enhancement that applies directly to the company LAN.

- **Get help from experts.** Dealers can often provide information on the best products for a given price. Chains also have in-house consultants that can assist you in planning your network, installing it and diagnosing any problems that may arise.

  Many network consultants can be found around larger cities. They can also help you plan, install and diagnose your network. When dealing with consultants, see if they've been certified by a national organization, and get references. Novell in particular has a very large program for certifying network engineers to work on NetWare networks throughout the country. It's called CNE, for Certified NetWare Engineer.

- **Test thoroughly.** Never install untested hardware or software. If necessary, hire consultants to research and test new products. If thorough testing is not possible without installing it on the network, install it when few people are using the system.

- **Make changes during off hours.** It's best to make changes in the network at night or over the weekend when no one is using it. If the change must be made during the day, check with the whole company or department to find a period of low demand.

- **Don't count on a new system to work right away.** If the new system must perform a critical task, keep the old system running until after working out all the problems with the new system. Canny administrators don't expect anything to work the first time.

Developing a Training Program

LAN administrators should help decide not only what, but also how users are taught. The more users know, the less support they will need later on and the more productive they will be. By participating in the training process, LAN administrators can ensure that users learn the information most relevant to the applications they will be using. Every group is different, but there are three levels of training that are appropriate for most network users:

- **Basic computing**—for computer novices who have little knowledge about using personal computers and know nothing about networks
- **Basic networking**—for those who can use computers but haven't used a network before
- **Applications and procedures**—for people who have used networks before but need to learn specific applications and procedures.

Assessing Users' Knowledge

Before developing a training program, a LAN administrator should carefully assess the users' skill levels to determine where the training process should begin. In many offices there's a wide variety of ability among users. Some need to start with training in basic computing; others may need only a run-through of various procedures.

A simple test can help divide a large group of diverse users into groups according to skill levels. The LAN administrator can then decide how each group should be trained. Test questions should be as straightforward and precise as possible. Groups of questions should be created for each of the three categories defined earlier: basic computing, basic networking and applications and procedures. That way users can be tested separately for each category. Direct questions that require a brief descriptive answer are most effective;

consider limiting responses to three sentences. Long, open-ended essay questions are generally not a good idea—there should be a clear right or wrong answer. But going too far the other way, with multiple choice or true/false questions, usually doesn't reveal the depth of a person's understanding. The test need not be a comprehensive exam in all network functions but should cover only the most basic concepts and ask questions only about really necessary knowledge. Users should be graded with a pass-fail system.

A SAMPLE TEST

Part One: Basic Computing

1. Identify all of the following components: CPU, keyboard, 5.25" disk drive, 3.5" disk drive, hard disk, mouse and monitor. [basic hardware knowledge]

2. Is a word processor a type of computer, a type of software or a human being? Briefly explain your answer. [the difference between hardware and software]

3. When you are working on the computer and you save your work, where does it go? [saving to disk]

4. How do you find out what files are on a disk? [basic operating system]

5. How do you change from a directory named DATA on drive C to a directory named DOCS that is also on drive C? [operating system navigational skills]

6. Describe the basic function of each of the following: word processor, database, spreadsheet, desktop publishing. [basic knowledge of major application software]

Part Two: Basic Networking

1. There is a high-performance computer in the corner office that is on all the time, but only the LAN administrator occasionally works on it. What is it for? [what and where the file server is]

2. How can two users on the network use the same word processing file without exchanging a floppy disk? [how the file server and shared directories work]

3. John hastily unplugged all the wires from the back of his computer and moved it from one side of the office to the other. What might John have done that is now preventing anyone from logging on to the network? [cabling]

4. John and Susan are working on the same network. Why is it that Susan can use the database and word processor, but John can only use the word processor? [different user configuration]

5. John and Susan are working on the same network, and a drive F shows up on both of their computers. Why doesn't John's drive F have the same files in it as Susan's drive F? [logical drives and user configuration]

6. Type the command for copying a file named FILE.TXT from drive H to a subdirectory named \DATA on drive C. [knowledge of operating system]

Part Three: Applications and Procedures

1. How do you send a printout from Lotus *1-2-3* to the HP LaserJet in accounting?

2. How would you use e-mail to send an urgent memo to everyone in customer service?

3. How do you check your mail and get rid of old messages?

4. What are the steps of the daily backup routine that must be performed by each department?

5. How do you assign a new customer number in the database?

6. How do you query orders that are more than three months old?

Learning in Groups

Users should be trained in groups whenever possible. Group training saves time and money. It also makes it easier to establish standard procedures and ensures that users are taught the same things at the same time.

In-House or Outside Training?

Network administrators can develop their own programs or use outside resources to train users. Most network vendors offer complete training programs. There are also specialized training companies and publishers that offer complete training programs, which may include courseware as well as computer- and video-based learning tools.

Quite often both the administrator and the network users have to be trained on the network immediately after installation.

Most LAN administrators use outside trainers and also train users themselves. Typically, they bring in outside help to provide a structured introduction to the network and specific applications, then train users themselves in procedures that are specific to the company or department.

Most users require some follow-up training to review details covered in the basic class. Even if the LAN administrator didn't conduct the class, he or she should know the material well enough to provide follow-up training.

Outside training is an especially good investment when no one in the office knows enough about a new technology. Quite often both the administrator and the network users have to be trained on the network immediately after installation. It may not be necessary to send all network users to outside training. If the administrator, a backup administrator and perhaps a few advanced users are trained, they can usually train other users.

Responding to Users

LAN administrators cannot do their jobs effectively unless they satisfy the network's users. LAN users frequently have the best ideas for new ways to use the LAN, but they sometimes lack the inclination to speak up. With only a little encouragement, LAN users can become a major force in determining the direction of the LAN. A successful LAN administrator must develop effective ways to solicit user feedback and respond to requests. Often this depends simply on the administrator's personality and ability to interact with people, but there are structured approaches that can help.

Meetings

If informal communications are inadequate, LAN administrators can conduct meetings or participate in existing meetings. In addition to providing the opportunity for brief training sessions, meetings can become open forums for discussing network issues.

A network steering committee that includes representatives from every department involved can help determine initial policies and define the role of the LAN administrator. The committee also offers feedback and suggestions on a continuing basis. Since it's impossible to predict exactly how much support a network will need, any plans the committee makes should anticipate change.

Service Request Forms

Many administrators use service request forms to make sure that they remember to do things people have asked for. Administrators who run large networks should rely on such forms to keep track of requests. These forms should be kept in a public place or circulated to all network users.

*Figure 7-1 A Sample
Service Request Form*

Service Request - Network Problem

Date: _____

1) Name: _____

2) Department: _____

3) Type of service requested:

      ☐ LocalTalk   ☐ Token ring

      ☐ Ethernet   ☐ Modem/dial-up

4) Type of machine and operating system:

    _____

5) Name for this machine:

    _____

6) Describe the problem:

    _____

    _____

    _____

    _____

    _____

    _____

    _____

    _____

Do not write below this line

Date report received: _____

Date problem assigned: _____

Date problem fixed: _____

Problem fixed by: _____

Reporting

Reporting is both a functional and a political tool. LAN administrators can gain a great deal of respect and credibility by simply explaining what's happening on the network and how well the network is running. This means different things in different organizations. LAN administrators should determine which specific network functions are most important to the organization and report on them, recording baseline levels and tracking improvements. Typical reports might go to the MIS director, the software coordinator, purchasing and supplies and the accounting department, so they can see who uses what and then allocate charges. Administrators should always be on the lookout for clear, quantifiable ways to note improvements in network performance.

Some types of tangible improvements that management can understand are a decrease in order-entry work hours with an increase of orders processed; reduced tape costs and fewer work hours spent swapping tapes with a new tape backup system; and faster response time for querying the customer database with the new database server. It's especially important to track the effects of changes made in the network so that successes can be documented.

Many—in fact, most—technical network performance statistics are boring and not meaningful to management. It's not very useful to keep them informed of the percentage of cache hits or other cryptic statistics. Instead, the data gathered from monitoring the network should be interpreted using nontechnical, meaningful terms. For instance, rather than mention cache hits, just explain that the server doesn't have enough memory or that the network is getting too big.

Most LAN administrators must file some type of status report with their manager on a weekly or monthly basis. Even if the boss doesn't ask for one, it's a good idea to submit one as often as possible—and retain a copy.

Status reports can vary from simple time sheets to narrative explanations. Narrative status reports are fine for reporting a few large tasks. But if a LAN administrator performs dozens of small tasks in a typical week, a report combining a written section and a chart may work better. The written section can describe longer, more complex projects and the chart can summarize tasks.

Budgeting

No matter how well performance is reported and time tracked, decision makers in management often judge the effectiveness of local area networks and their administrators by the bottom line: cost. Most LAN administrators have to submit some type of annual budget. Administrators who submit clear, detailed and accurate budgets are going to gain respect and greater influence with management.

Some creative interpretation of budget data can also help put a favorable spin on network costs.

Costs are difficult to predict, but with careful record keeping and by comparing projected costs with actual costs, LAN administrators can learn to write realistic budgets. Some creative interpretation of budget data can also help put a favorable spin on network costs. By assigning network costs to company profit centers, for example, LAN administrators can show how the network is helping the company make money.

Budgets consist of two main parts: fixed and discretionary. The fixed budget includes the items that are already committed to, such as maintenance contracts for the current network, salaries, leased data lines, off-site data storage and so on. Discretionary items include one-time costs and future plans: new equipment and software, new network support people and any costs other than simply maintaining the existing network.

Network Management Tools

These systems, usually made up of hardware and software components, offer a graphic look at all or parts of a network, from both a physical and statistical point of view.

Servers, workstations, cabling, bridges, gateways; sophisticated systems software that moves the data around and controls the operation; specific application software that helps you do whatever needs doing, whether it be using a database, communications, word processing, printing—there are many, many potential elements in a LAN system, proportional to how large a staff you have and how many jobs are running concurrently. Keeping track of all this calls for LAN management software, single-task or integrated network management software systems that can both monitor and diagnose every aspect of your daily work. It offers a graphic roadmap of your LAN's components, providing a wide range of information you can use to find out exactly what's going on around the network, including utilities that specialize in these areas:

- **File and Directory Management.** Helping you navigate the maze of directories and files of the file server's disk; getting an overview of the server's directory structure and allowing you to control everything stored on the hard disk of your LANs; providing special menuing and archiving capability

- **Usage Monitoring.** Telling a manager which applications are being used, who is using them, for how long and from which workstations

- **Traffic Monitoring.** Allowing you to measure data such as time spent at a specific task and how much work is flowing past a certain point; recording and reporting traffic to and from workstations, displaying specific problems throughout the system

- **Accounting.** Reporting and allocating the cost of your network to specific users in the system

- **Troubleshooting.** Reporting and correcting equipment on the blink; setting off alarms when there are network errors

■ **Security.** Restricting access, recording user activities and auditing data; also providing file locking to protect unattended workstations and file encryption, which creates passwords to keep out unauthorized users.

The more complex the LAN, the more sophisticated a LAN management software system is needed.

Network product vendors have begun to offer what can rightfully be called *integrated* network management systems, stations, centers or managers. They're integrated because they combine many management capabilities—from performance monitoring to audit-trail accounting to changing configuration parameters—in one package.

Traditionally, network management products have been divided into five categories:

■ Security management (or variations of password-protection schemes)
■ Performance management (monitoring network capacity and loading)
■ Accounting (audit trail) management (capturing and allocating costs of the network to network users)
■ Fault management (troubleshooting, finding and correcting failing equipment)
■ Configuration management (network installation, booting, tracking hardware/software configurations).

Providing as many of these capabilities as possible in one software package is the goal of vendors offering integrated network management systems. These systems, usually made up of hardware and software components, offer a graphic look at all or parts of a network, from both a physical and statistical point of view. They generally overlay the LAN's components on a geographical or logical map displayed on a color graphics monitor. They also provide a wide range of statistical information the LAN manager can use to find out what's going on around the network, and then reconfigure the LAN's components to avoid trouble.

An integrated network management product, unlike the myriad standalone applications available, could automatically tell a LAN manager that a server or remote bridge is overworked, then allow taking that component out of operation, changing its operating parameters and putting it back into service. It could also let the manager see how many bad packets are crossing an Ethernet network—thus slowing it down—or set danger thresholds that automatically beep or display an on-screen message when a network component is experiencing trouble or about to fail.

Protocol Analyzers

Since all network operating systems depend on the use of protocols, many problems with networks can be isolated using protocol analyzers. Protocol analyzers come in two forms—either software that can be installed on an appropriate computer (i.e., one with an Ethernet or token ring interface card) or hardware that includes built-in software for analyzing protocols. Triticom's *LANdecoder/e* for DOS computers and AG Group's *EtherPeek* for Macs are examples of software protocol analyzers, while Network General's Sniffer is an example of a hardware protocol analyzer.

Protocol analyzers are not usually designed for the first-time network manager, since they do expect the manager to understand what protocols are being transmitted on the network and how different protocols relate to each other. (A simple network session between two computers can easily involve five or six protocols.) Protocol analyzers monitor the network continuously and determine what each packet contains. Once these packets are stored within the analyzer, a user can investigate what protocols are being used and what network nodes are transmitting and receiving the packets. This information can be particularly helpful in determining whether a workstation has been misconfigured or why one client-server pair is operating less efficiently than another.

But making sense of a long list of network packets and the protocols involved can be an onerous task, even for an experienced analyst. Some vendors have realized this and now add artificial intelligence to their protocol analyzers. These AI analyzers can then isolate and identify network problems more readily than before. (Examples are Network General's Expert Sniffer and Hewlett-Packard's Network Advisor.) Also, there are other network tools that can help pinpoint a network problem without the use of protocol analysis, which are discussed next.

Network Monitoring

Aside from worrying about physical problems such as broken cables or faulty connectors and interface cards, a primary concern for network managers is maintaining adequate network performance for their users. Monitoring tools can be a particularly effective aid in this task. Rather than show each packet's contents, monitors present lists or (better yet) graphic displays of the number of packets transmitted over time as well as the amount of network traffic exchanged between pairs of nodes on the network. The first display gives an idea of "crunch times" for network usage and can also assist in planning for major upgrades to the network. The second display, representing paired traffic, can alert administrators to heavy users of servers (or other network resources). Also, misconfigured workstations or faulty interface cards can often be recognized by the excessive amount of network traffic they generate.

Newer network monitors also include alerts and various ways for notifying a network manager about network problems. With the increasing size and complexity of LANs, these options are becoming increasingly necessary. The administrator who has collected some data on how the network performs under normal conditions can set alert levels in the monitoring program so that traffic exceeding those levels is displayed in red, for example. The most basic alerts are simply sounds or alert boxes displayed on the screen, but more advanced systems can also send e-mail or even page the administrator on a beeper. The most sophisticated systems can work through a hierarchy of network managers with different alert forms depending on the severity of the problem or the length of time it goes unattended.

Some examples are Frye's *NetWare Early Warning System*, which is restricted to use on NetWare networks, and Caravelle Software's *NetWORKS*, which can use a Macintosh computer to monitor AppleTalk, IPX and TCP/IP networks.

Network Mappers

Network mapping tools cannot solve many network problems by themselves. But having the ability to draw a map of the network automatically can be a plus for visualizing potential problems, for planning for future expansion or for reporting.

One occasion when network maps can be used as a diagnostic tool is when a group of users loses network access. A map might quickly show that all affected users are connected to the backbone at the same point (a wiring hub, for example), or that they're all passing traffic through the same bridge or router. Some mapping utilities permit comparing a new map to an older map that has been stored. This makes it easier to see who's been affected by a network fault, since disconnected nodes do not show up on the newer map.

Novell's new Network Management System includes a network mapping program, as does Visisoft's Enterprise Systems Platform. Farallon offers NetAtlas as part of its network management package for Macs.

Hub Controllers

The development of intelligent hubs over the last few years has made them increasingly important linchpins in network architectures. The added computing power that resides within the hubs makes them ideal candidates for collecting network statistics. Many of the newer network management systems are designed to use intelligent hubs as a major factor in managing networks. Some examples are Synoptics' *LattisNet* and Cabletron's *Spectrum*. Not incidentally, both Synoptics and Cabletron are the market leaders in the sales of intelligent hubs.

"People are paying more attention to hardware and software inventories mainly because it's one of the easiest places to control costs. If you know what is where, you can optimize the usage of what you already have."

—LIZ BROSS, SABER SOFTWARE

Many vendors offer hubs with their own control software, but these proprietary systems can only make the job more difficult for network managers who must manage a network composed of hubs from a variety of vendors. A much better decision is to purchase only hubs that include Simple Network Management Protocol (SNMP) management agents and therefore can be queried and controlled by SNMP-based management software (such as Synoptics' *LattisNet*, Cabletron's *Spectrum* and Sun's *SunNet Manager*). SNMP has become an ad hoc standard for network management, and most vendors either actively provide SNMP support or plan to provide it in the future.

The larger vendors also offer modular hubs, which can contain bridges and routers as well as wiring hubs. Since these additional network devices can also be controlled by SNMP, it becomes increasingly important that all devices can be controlled by SNMP.

Network Auditing and Inventorying

Sometimes solving network problems is more a function of what software the users are running than what cabling, connectors, hubs or servers the network uses. Network inventory tools can help maintain an up-to-date list of what software users are running.

All the inventory programs work in pretty much the same way. They either poll the user's workstation to see what's running or check a server containing shared software to see which user is running software from the server. (The Mac operating system includes support for detailed polling, so that Mac-based inventory tools can tell the manager what fonts, applications and desk accessories are being used as well as details regarding hard disks, monitors and interface cards.)

Some examples of inventorying programs are Brightwork Development's *LAN Automatic Inventory* and Magee Enterprises' *Network HQ* for NetWare networks, along with ON Technology's *Status*Mac* and Technology Works' *GraceLAN*.

Conclusion

There are many tools that you can use to manage small as well as large LANs. The well-equipped network manager should include protocol analyzers, monitoring tools, configuration tools (such as for hubs) as well as audit or inventory tools. Not all these tools can work together yet, so it will be the manager's job to coordinate the use of the tools and create reports combining their results to help isolate problems and maintain a well-performing network.

SNMP-based tools are increasing in number, and SNMP is rapidly becoming an integrating factor in network management. As SNMP evolves, using SNMP-based tools will only make that job easier.

Response Time for Network Disaster

When planning for network disaster recoveries, you need to assign acceptable downtimes for each group of users (HQ, managers, accounting, etc.). Perhaps a better term than downtime is your reaction time. The question you are really asking is more like this: "How fast should you and your organization react to a failure of a particular group's network, such as the executive e-mail users?"

8 / LAN Security

A significant network failure can cause major problems for any operation. Nevertheless, such breakdowns inevitably occur. Cables wear out or get disconnected, hard disks develop bad sectors and lose data, computers malfunction, users accidentally delete or overwrite their files, printers jam, equipment is stolen, buildings burn down. LANs are vulnerable to many threats, and LAN users and administrators must prepare for as many of them as possible.

While it may not be possible to calculate risk precisely, the more we know about and are prepared for potential threats, the less likely it is that we'll have a disastrous loss of data or function on our network. Careful planning and prevention can reduce known perils, such as component failure, environmental threat, theft and software problems. Each protective measure we take is an important step for network security.

Dealing With Disaster

To understand how important the network is to the organization's operations, LAN administrators should first try to estimate what is at risk from a network failure. The importance of the data, the loss of functions that may be critical to operations and lost prestige are just some of the factors to consider in quantifying potential losses. This process will help focus efforts and use available funds more effectively.

Lost Data

The data that workers have entered is probably the most valuable and irreplaceable part of the system. To set a value on this data, the administrator must consider the cost of recreating the data and the cost of lost revenue the data was expected to produce.

"We've had security on mainframes since the get-go. With the move to networks, we're exposing business resources we had under lock and key."

—Bob Bales, International Computer Security Association

Different types of data have vastly different values. The loss of data from a noncritical application may be only a minor inconvenience. The loss of data from a mission-critical application can be disastrous. Every LAN administrator should know the importance of all the data stored on the network. If they don't know this already, they should ask all the department heads to explain the importance of the data they use and how it fits into the general operations of the organization.

Administrators must know whether or not various types of data are recoverable. This depends on the application. If the company receives orders by mail and keeps the paper orders for a certain time, then the data for that period is completely recoverable. If it takes orders by phone and enters them directly into a computer, then recent orders may not be recoverable. The estimate of the cost of data loss must take this into account. If the company can recreate all the data, the only cost is the data-entry time; if not, the loss includes the original data-entry time as well as the potential revenue associated with the data.

If a firm makes reliable backup copies of its data every day, its risk exposure is at most between 8 and 24 hours of data-entry time and the revenue that might have been generated by that data. If this cost justifies additional protection methods, top management should know.

Lost Functions and Personnel Costs

If a power interruption, cable failure or similar problem shuts down the LAN—even if no data is lost and nothing goes wrong with the software—the company will lose money. The actual functioning of the LAN has a certain economic value. If the LAN performs a critical function in company operations, then every minute that LAN is not working may cause a permanent revenue loss. The company not only loses business, but it must pay employees to sit and wait for the system to be repaired.

To get a rough idea of how much LAN downtime will cost your company, add up the hourly wages of every employee who depends on the LAN to do his or her job, then add this figure to the revenue loss from lost data.

A simple calculation might look like this:

$4,500	Hourly labor cost
$11,000	Average revenue per hour
$15,500	Cost per hour of LAN downtime

There are sophisticated spreadsheets that can more precisely calculate the cost of network downtime, taking into account such factors as company revenue and the size of the network.

Lost Prestige

This area is hardest to quantify, but it does have a direct effect on revenues. For companies in a competitive line of business, reliability is a key factor to success. Most company heads have an intuitive sense of how many service failures customers will tolerate before taking their business elsewhere.

If network downtime can prevent the company from serving its customers, LAN administrators should make it clear to top management how many customers may be lost for each day the LAN is out of commission. This can help them get additional resources for protective measures.

Repair and Replacement Costs

Repair and replacement costs vary depending on what type of service agreement and insurance a company has. With a service contract, potential repairs are paid for ahead of time. A predictable cost is better than gambling that no big expensive problem will occur. A service contract that guarantees a short response time can also save a lot of money in the long run. Service contracts are really an insurance policy against unexpected repair costs.

Administrators who do not have a service contract should try to estimate the number of repairs and service calls that might be necessary and include that figure in their budgets. In the next section, we look at ways to predict when hardware is likely to wear out and fail.

A good insurance policy should provide for the replacement of equipment if it's stolen. Some types of business insurance cover data loss, paying for the data-entry time needed to recreate data.

Number of Anticipated Losses

There's no completely accurate way to calculate the amount or number of losses that might occur from network failures. But it is not too hard to get a rough idea of what to expect and how to reduce the chances of serious problems. The information learned about the cost of potential losses will focus company resources on the greatest threats to the network and organization. Any list of these threats would include network component failure.

Preparing for Component Failure

The most common threat to all networks is the failure of network components. Fortunately, it's also the easiest to prepare for. Hard disks, disk controllers, network servers, cabling, network interface cards and workstations will all eventually fail, causing some type of problem on the network. Equipment has become more reliable over the years, but this sometimes lulls LAN administrators into a false sense of security. Failures still occur, and even if they occur less often, they are just as serious.

Hard disks, disk controllers, network servers, cabling, network interface cards and workstations will all eventually fail.

Many network component manufacturers supply an estimate of the mean time between failure (MTBF), especially for hard disks. These numbers can be used to estimate the likelihood of network hardware failure in a given period of time. For example, a LAN administrator may want to know the likely number of hardware failures for a three-year period of continuous operation. For each component, divide the MTBF into 1 to determine the number of failures per hour, and then multiply that number by 26,280 (the number of hours in 3 years). The calculation for a hard disk with an MTBF of 20,000 hours would look like this:

.00005 x 26,280 = 1.314

In other words, the hard disk is likely to fail 1.3 times over 3 years of continuous operation. Repeating this calculation for every critical network component and then adding the number of failures yields some idea of the number of failures to expect. The failure of a single workstation usually does not cause network downtime. Calculations should use only the figures from critical components. A simple calculation might look something like this:

MTBF	Component
0.875	File server
1.971	Hard disk subsystem
0.657	File server network adapter
<u>0.329</u>	Network cable system
3.832	Total failure in 3 years

These figures are helpful in establishing basic guidelines, but they should not be taken too literally. They indicate when the hardware is likely to fail if nothing else goes wrong first. People planning network protection schemes should keep track of various MTBF figures and the age of each component. However, this is only a first step. The system does not take into account how serious the failure will be. Some failures may destroy the component, while others may be hardly noticeable. There are also many unpredictable hazards caused by human error, acts of God and software problems.

Most LAN administrators use a combination of record keeping, calculating the MTBF, performance monitoring and intuition to decide when to replace old hardware. Learning from the experiences of other users and vendors is also very helpful. The older the equipment is, the more useful network management tools and diagnostic utilities are in making sure it's working properly.

For critical applications where failures can cost thousands of dollars, hardware redundancy can make a network more fault-tolerant. Redundant hardware—another computer or hard disk—duplicates the function of a primary device and takes over if the primary device fails. Most network operating systems allow redundant hard disks to be set up on file servers; some even provide for entirely redundant file servers.

Preparing for Environmental Threats

The environment of the network includes nearly everything except the system itself and its users. Heat, air quality, cleanliness, quality of the electrical service and proximity to other hazards can all affect the reliability of a network.

Generally, if a human being is comfortable in an environment, the LAN will also thrive.

The computers used in LANs were usually designed for desktop use and are therefore quite sturdy and reliable. The type of environmentally controlled computer room required by a mainframe is usually not needed for a LAN file server. If you already have a controlled computer room, go ahead and use it. But generally, if a human being is comfortable in an environment, the LAN will also thrive.

Important LAN components should be kept in a well-heated or air-conditioned room, depending on the climate. Computers should be at least 6 inches away from the wall so that air can circulate properly and prevent overheating. Keep the equipment clean, occasionally checking inside for dust buildup, which can cause overheating and short-circuiting.

Electrical Problems

Electrical failures are one of the most common causes of system failure. There are four main types of electrical problems that can cause failures:

- Transients or spikes—periods of high voltage that last for a short time
- Power surges—periods of high voltage that last longer than transients
- Brownouts—periods of reduced voltage
- Blackouts—complete losses of power

Figure 8-1 The Four Main Types of Electrical Problems

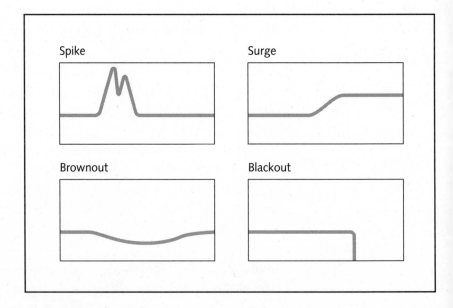

Most power companies have a few of these failures every year. A reliable network must prepare for them. If possible, crucial network components, like file servers, should be isolated on their own electrical circuits. Power-hungry devices, such as refrigerators and electric heaters, can cause sudden voltage drops in a circuit when they switch on and power surges when they turn off. File servers shouldn't share a circuit with such appliances.

There are two devices used to protect against electrical problems: line conditioners and uninterruptible power supplies.

If the file server is suddenly turned off by a power failure, all the information stored in RAM is lost, and files can be left open and corrupted.

Line conditioners filter excess voltage during transients and power surges and also even out low power conditions. Every important network component should use a line conditioner. An effective one must be able to handle up to 10,000 volts and have a response time of 2 nanoseconds. Many low-cost line conditioners don't meet these standards. The prices of good computer line conditioners start at around $50.

If the file server is suddenly turned off by a power failure, all the information stored in RAM is lost, and files can be left open and corrupted. Most network operating systems can recover from sudden shutdowns with minimal losses, but for critical applications, an uninterruptible power supply (UPS) can be a lifesaver. The UPS, which is a box that plugs into the wall, keeps systems running for a limited time during brownouts and blackouts. It usually contains several standard electrical outlets to which one can connect other devices. Power is fed into the UPS, which in turn powers the computer system. When normal power shuts off, the UPS continues to supply battery power to the computer system long enough for it to be shut down normally or for a generator to take over. Most UPSes also include a surge suppressor and other power conditioners that protect the quality of the electricity fed to the computer system.

Different UPSes have different power capacities (how much power they can deliver for how long) and other features. When choosing a UPS, consider how many devices it needs to support and how long it takes either to shut down the system or to start a generator. UPSes cost anywhere from a few hundred to several thousand dollars, depending on capacities and features.

Accidents and Acts of God

Floods, fires, hurricanes, earthquakes, freak accidents—these types of events are hard to predict, although any preparation is helpful. If your area is subject to any type of troublesome climatic or geological event (and most areas are), you should take all possible precautions, including developing a disaster recovery plan that can be put into action immediately.

LAN Disaster Recovery Plan for World Wide Products Inc.

In the event of a calamity that damages or destroys our office and/or a significant portion of our network, the network recovery team will move into action. Landra Tankha will serve as coordinator. If she is not available, a new coordinator will be selected according to the order of the list below.

Team members	Home phone
Landra Tankha	555-3455
Peter Rinzler	555-3454
Lisa Feldstein	555-2343
Michelle Morley	555-2344

If none of these people is available, contact Vanstar at (333) 555-3434.

Restoring the Network

Top Priority: We must restore the order entry and accounting systems with at least 12 workstations within 48 hours.

The LAN recovery coordinator will report to the office as soon as possible, conduct an initial survey of the damage, and contact the other members of the team. The LAN recovery coordinator will report on progress and take additional orders from the companywide recovery coordinator.

If the Office is Destroyed

If our office space is not usable, we will temporarily move to our distribution center in Oakland. All recovery team members should report to the distribution center by 9:00 a.m. of the next business day, even if no one has contacted them.

Replacing Equipment

Vanstar has a detailed list of the equipment we need in order to restore minimal operations.

Tasks

A team member will be responsible for a specific task or group of tasks.

Coordinator:

- Assess damage to existing equipment, note condition of every CPU and printer
- Purchase replacement equipment sufficient to restore minimal operations defined above
- Move equipment to new location (if necessary)
- Assign unanticipated tasks to other team members

Peter:

- Retrieve off-site backups (if necessary)
- Restore file server and check configuration

Michelle and Lisa:

- Restore or install cabling
- Connect workstations to network and make sure they work correctly

If any of these people are not available, the coordinator will reassign tasks.

Additional precautions that you should take include using fireproof storage boxes for backup tapes (even off-site backup tapes), keeping file servers on the second or higher floor to avoid flooding damage, checking the seismic safety of your building, bracing and securing all furniture holding network equipment and checking for anything that could fall onto equipment. Anything else you can think of is probably a good idea as well.

Hardware Theft

Many companies protect themselves against sophisticated computer crackers and rogue users but overlook the disgruntled employee or the burglar who walks off with some crucial piece of valuable equipment. Hardware theft is one of the most disastrous threats to a network. To determine the probability of theft, you should ask yourself a few questions:

- Are there many visitors to your site on a regular basis? If so, you should establish a system of signing in and out, issue passes and possibly even require escorts.

- Do some people work after hours or on weekends? This increases the risk of employee theft and makes people less likely to report off-hour activity in the office.

- Is there a high incidence of computer theft, and theft in general, where your organization is located? Check the crime statistics.

In addition to such traditional security methods as guards and alarm systems, try to think of any other methods that will make it difficult to get equipment out of the office, such as engraved serial numbers, electronic trackers and physical anchors.

Preparing for Threats to Software and Data

User error, user malice and software problems can pose a significant threat to a LAN. These threats may seem more intangible and unpredictable than hardware threats, but they're just as serious. Preventive measures can greatly reduce the danger posed by these problems.

Preventing Software Problems

Software failures can be just as serious as hardware failures. Software design flaws, or bugs, can damage data files, causing disastrous losses if current backups aren't available. The initial release of a new software package often contains more flaws than mature versions that have been in use for some time. Updates to previously reliable programs can introduce new problems, especially if new features are added. There's no meaningful way to quantify the likelihood of software errors, but the newer the software, the more careful users should be. This applies not only to application software, but also to network operating systems. As when installing any new LAN component, rigorous testing can reveal any serious problems before they have a chance to actually cause harm.

Restricting Users

Users are a major source of network problems. Most problems are caused by errors, but there are occasional experiments that go awry or acts of deliberate sabotage. Every leading network operating system lets the LAN administrator create user profiles that define exactly what rights each user has on the network and what data he or she can access. An effective LAN administrator grants these rights cautiously. If users don't need access to a certain directory, for example, it shouldn't even appear in their configuration. The less they can see, the less they will want. When using groups to assign user rights, make sure that no group possesses rights that any member of the group should not have.

Be sure to use the network's password protection scheme. Most systems provide for automatic password expiration and renewal. After a certain period of time, usually about 60 days, the user must enter a new password. This prevents anyone who inadvertently learned an old password from continuing to use the network.

Administrators may also want to restrict the time when users can log in to the network. Most operating systems allow this. If users should not be able to use the system after normal working hours, it can be specified in their user profile that they can log in only between certain hours.

Data Profiles

Most network operating systems let the administrator define whether specific data files are read-only, read-write or shareable. Read-only data can be used but not changed. Important program files are usually marked as read-only. Read-write data can be modified by any user. Data files and documents are usually read-write. The appropriate permissions can ensure that specific files aren't overwritten. A shareable file can be used by more than one person at the same time. If the network has single-user applications, it's very important to define all the program files as nonshareable. If two people try to use a single-user application at the same time, they both may crash and the program files may be corrupted.

Data Theft

As LANs become more critical to company operations, they're used to store and process more valuable information. Many LAN administrators are responsible for protecting data that could be worth millions of dollars to competitors. In addition to physical security and password protection, they can apply even more advanced measures to protect against data theft.

Encryption is the process of scrambling data into a form that's unintelligible to unauthorized users. Encryption protects data on a network that's being sent through a cable or stored on a file server hard disk. Online encryption boxes or boards can be installed on every computer in the network. The system is completely transparent to users, yet all the data sent through the cabling and stored on the file server is encrypted. Other encryption schemes consist entirely of software.

Many LAN administrators are responsible for protecting data that could be worth millions of dollars to competitors.

Diskless workstations—PCs without floppy disk drives—are less expensive than standard PCs and are also more secure. Because they don't have floppy drives, they can't be used to copy data off the network.

All data cables transmitting electricity also emit radio waves that can be picked up by intercept equipment near the cable. Shielded cable can reduce these transmissions, but ordinary shielded cable doesn't always eliminate the possibility. Special shielded conduits are available that meet government security standards.

Fiber-optic cable uses light instead of electricity, so it transmits no radio waves. Because fiber-optic cable is also very hard to tap physically, it's ideal for security purposes.

Virus Protection

Viruses are becoming a larger problem with each passing year. But many LAN administrators take no action against viruses until their systems become infected.

Viruses are programs capable of replicating themselves and causing various degrees of mischief. They're spread through floppy disks, bulletin board systems, mainframe systems and, of course, LANs. Some viruses are relatively harmless; others can be disastrous, destroying directories, deleting files and causing software crashes, bad sectors and unbootable hard disks.

There are several diagnostic tools capable of detecting various virus infections and repairing the damage. If a system is infected by a virus for which no cure is yet available, administrators may have to perform a low-level reformat on all network hard disks, reinstall the software from the write-protected master disks and restore data from the most recent backup.

Prevention is the best approach for avoiding virus damage. Once it's discovered, an infection has probably already done damage. Here are some useful preventive measures:

- Don't allow users to install any software on the network.
- Teach users to be very wary of floppy disks. If they must use floppy disks, have them use diagnostic software to scan all floppies first. Also consider using diskless workstations.
- Install software on the network only from sealed boxes.
- Make sure that all master program disks are write-protected and that every workstation has a write-protected startup disk.

Managing Network Security

Two areas of security must be managed on networks. The first area is at the level of network management. This level involves restricting LAN access to network managers for such activities as configuring routers and assigning file-server passwords. A second level involves maintaining the security of the users and their data.

9 / The Networked Workplace

Reengineering Businesses with LANs
Network Administrators
Planning a LAN

In the old mainframe environment, the primary aim of both business owners and departmental managers was to automate existing procedures. Computerizing was the word everybody used to describe the approach. LANs are the next step in the evolution of business automation. Rather than simply computerizing old ways of doing things, LANs allow their owners and users to pioneer new ways of performing tasks and handling information. This is often called reengineering.

Reengineering Businesses with LANs

The main thrust of reengineering is to treat individual employees as generalists rather than as specialists with limited knowledge. Thus a team of coworkers can attack and solve a problem one month and those same workers may be on different teams solving other problems the following month. It's a change in the process of business, more so than merely altering the business organization. For example, a group of designers and editors in a publishing house might first design a new book using e-mail and screen-sharing utilities. Then, once that project's under way, the designers work among themselves to finish the artwork for the next issue of a magazine while the editors are using e-mail and a group-editing program to prepare the first draft of another book.

Crucial to these themes of employee generalists and self-empowered teams is a freer flow of important business data, ready access to that data, and flexibility in how the teams work. That's where LANs come into play.

Centralized Data, Decentralized Processing

One of a LAN's key advantages is its ability to offer access to centralized data via decentralized processing. In a nutshell, this means that LAN users can use personalized applications to easily work with a centralized repository of information. For example, one might choose to use a favorite spreadsheet program at the workstation to analyze sales data acquired from the company's central database.

Many small companies, such as law firms, accounting firms, retail businesses and medical practices, must deal with large amounts of information—data that can't be stored on standalone PCs efficiently or effectively. A LAN offers the perfect way of giving users access to key data in a cost-effective manner.

Easier Access to Information

Even when everyone in a company has access to the important databases of the company, finding the information that's crucial to closing a sale, or perhaps market intelligence about a competitor, isn't easy. And with more information arising every day, the task isn't getting any easier.

Companies can use client-server technology to simplify such information access by using smarter front-end tools on the users' workstations. These tools include programs for generating queries and reports, Executive Information Systems (EISes), program development tools as well as some of the latest business application software.

> *"E-mail, news feeds, computer conferences, bulletin boards and online databases all require that you wade through a deluge of electronic data."*
>
> —LAURE ROWAN, NETWORK MANAGER, FORTUNE 100 FIRM

The latest generation of query and report tools allows users to graphically define queries for data and let database programmers construct queries and distribute them to users. The more user-defined customizability that's put on the user's workstation, the easier it can be for users to decide what data they need and how to find it. Some examples include *ClearAccess*, *Quest* and *PersonalAccess*.

For example, the VP of Sales might use *Forest and Trees* to access and plot regional sales data for the last quarter, or Microsoft's *Office Information Pack* along with *Excel* to manipulate and plot the sales data. Tools like *PowerBuilder* and *ClearAccess* can be used by database programmers to create SQL-based queries, which can then be distributed (via e-mail, for example) to the appropriate users to acquire needed data from mainframe-resident databases. This is especially useful if users are accessing the same type of data from month to month (such as sales data). The type of manager who has to explore the data by digging deeper into sales or customer reports might turn to tools like *Q+E* or *DataPrism*.

Many of the current EIS programs require programming (or at least setup) by someone who's knowledgeable about the structure of the corporate databases and where the pertinent data resides. A main advantage of EIS programs is their graphical interface to reams of data and user-definable charts and tables once they get the data they need. Some examples of EIS software are *Forest and Trees*, *Commander*, *EIS Pack* and *LightShip*.

"The key question always is which information to look for in order to make your business run smoothly and to control it."

—HANS ELZAS,
MANAGING
DIRECTOR,
SOFTWARE
CONNECTION B.V.,
THE NETHERLANDS

Although query software helps users find important data more easily, newer generations of query software (especially SQL front ends; see Chapter 5, LAN Applications) now work seamlessly with existing applications, such as word processors, spreadsheets and graphing software. By adding this power to familiar software, the learning curve for handling queries is reduced and the user can comfortably deal with new sources of data within a familiar program. Some examples are databases like *Paradox* and *Access* as well as the best-selling spreadsheets, Lotus *1-2-3* and Microsoft *Excel*.

Front-end software can be helpful regardless of how the data is stored. Thus front-end software can be particularly useful for a company that is moving data from a mainframe- or minicomputer-based database to a distributed database. In fact, front-end software's utility becomes even greater as companies switch to distributed databases because the software can make it easier to locate relevant data.

Fast Transaction Processing

Online transaction processing (OLTP), involving several users accessing and altering a database, has traditionally been handled by computer systems based on minicomputer or mainframe hardware. But technological advances (faster PCs, improved operating systems and database management software) are resulting in more OLTP systems based on PC LANs. A client-server LAN can achieve the concurrency and data-integrity necessary for OLTP with such features as record locking, transaction logging and crash recovery.

Companies such as Information Builders, Informix Software, Progress Software, Data Access and Gupta Technologies make powerful versions of LAN software that offer reliable and reproducible connections between front ends and distributed databases.

With a mainframe or minicomputer, a user's process resides on the same machine as the database engine, receives only the data it needs and locks other processes only out of records actually being updated. A client-server LAN does all this by having the server send only the records requested by a client application, thereby reducing network traffic and keeping locked records to a minimum.

Recently, PC-class hardware has begun to offer minicomputer-level performance, thanks to faster and more capable microprocessors. Meanwhile, OS/2 and Novell NetWare 386 are providing an industry-standard operating system and network environment for advanced database servers. The combination is proving a powerful boost to LAN-based OLTP technology.

Standardizing E-Mail

Along with the ability to share files and peripherals, one of LAN technology's strongest features is its electronic mail (e-mail) support. Of the numerous electronic mail software packages on the market, most conform to an industry standard developed by Action Technologies called Message Handling Service (MHS). A family of CCITT standards goes under the title of X.400.

"Failure to adopt a standards approach to information technologies is likely to lead to a patchwork environment high on diversity but low on functionality."

— DAVE MOLTA, SYRACUSE UNIVERSITY

E-Mail With MHS

MHS is a utility that carries out e-mail addressing, transportation and delivery functions. The standard's philosophy and structure might be compared to that of the U.S. Postal Service—although it's tempting to say that MHS does its work faster and more efficiently.

It's difficult to overstate the value of MHS to LAN e-mail technology. Without the existence of standards, LAN users running different e-mail packages wouldn't be able to exchange messages easily or reliably. MHS is so important because of its widespread acceptance—it is currently supported by Novell NetWare, Banyan

VINES, 3Com 3+Share, Microsoft LAN Manager and many other products and companies.

MHS provides three layers: a directory manager, a connectivity manager and a transport manager. The directory manager provides a routing table with the names and addresses of the users, hosts and workgroups in its domain. But the directory manager is not a true manager because it doesn't actively manage anything. It's a repository where configuration and routing information is stored. The network administrator manages routing tables manually.

The simplest and least expensive way to connect field staffers to their LAN is with remote control software and a modem.

The next layer, the connectivity manager, manages the coordination of the local e-mail application with the MHS system. The connectivity manager provides a way for programmers to write applications to communicate with MHS. Operating at each host computer, it regularly looks for incoming messages. If the message is for a local user, the connectivity manager delivers it to a local mailbox. If the message is for a remote user, the connectivity manager consults the routing table and, if all is well, leaves it for the transport manager to deliver to a remote host or gateway.

What if you had 50 pieces of e-mail for delivery to a distant site? MHS's connectivity manager looks at the routing of the messages awaiting shipment and bundles those "envelopes" into a single packet for shipment, eliminating most of the overhead required for transmission. When the packet arrives at its destination, MHS "bursts" it open to reveal and extract the envelopes for routing to local users or rebundles it for forwarding elsewhere.

X.400 Support

X.400 is an international e-mail interexchange standard recognized by the CCITT that encompasses an entire field of standards, since the designation by itself only defines the way an e-mail message is addressed. X.401, for example, describes basic intersystem service elements, and X.411 defines message transfer protocols. But when LAN experts and other people say "X.400," they're usually talking about the entire category of CCITT e-mail standards.

Compared to MHS, X.400 is more powerful and complex. That's also its main drawback, since X.400 tends to be so costly to implement that only commercial e-mail service providers and large corporations with networks spanning states and continents tend to use it. Still, since the X.400 designation pops up in vendor literature and other LAN documents, you should be familiar with the term.

Although X.400 has had its start with international e-mail, it's now grown in popularity with corporations seeking a way to tie together different types of LAN-based e-mail. These companies turn to X.400 as the corporate e-mail backbone and tie in the other e-mail systems via e-mail gateways. Every major e-mail vendor now offers such X.400 gateways for its systems.

Sales Force Automation

LANs usually bring to mind the image of networked desktop workstations in a conventional office, but they can also be used to connect to workers who are working in hotel rooms, client sites and other field locations. With notebook computers now a standard-issue item for most sales representatives and other field workers, it's only natural to allow these people access to your LAN.

The simplest and least expensive way to connect field staffers to their LAN is with remote control software and a modem. The user uses the software to dial up a modem-equipped workstation on the LAN that is also equipped with remote control software. The user can then control the workstation from a hotel room, for example, with all of the screen and keyboard activity mirrored on the notebook computer. The big drawback is response time, particularly in the area of screen redraws; at 2,400 bps the process is slow. But the approach is quite inexpensive and suitable for checking databases, filing orders and reading e-mail from just about anywhere in the world with a telephone.

An alternative is to install a network-oriented modem, such as the NetModem/E model made by Shiva Corp. The device installs directly into AppleTalk and IPX LANs and is dedicated to providing remote access. It provides 9,600-bps operation with V.32bis and V.42bis support. The unit connects to standard Ethernet cabling. As with an ordinary modem, performance won't be nearly as fast as using a workstation on-site, due to the inherent speed limitations of voice-grade telephone lines, which have a narrow bandwidth.

Of the employees who have the option to telecommute, fewer than 10 percent take advantage of the offer.

High-volume communication needs may be met with a dedicated access server, such as the type supported by Novell's NetWare, NetWare SNA Access. Assigning a 386 or better PC the task of managing several simultaneous communications sessions with remote users will allow the LAN to offer relatively rapid access; the applications actually function inside the access server.

Telecommuting

Travelers Insurance, U.S. West, IBM, New York Life Insurance, J.C. Penney and the states of California, Washington and Florida all have one thing in common—they permit selected staffers to telecommute to work by connecting into a LAN.

Telecommuting—the practice of allowing employees, as well as independent contractors, to connect and interact with host computers, permitting employees to work offsite full- or part-time via computer—is a relatively new trend. The New York market research company Link Resources puts the number of telecommuters in the U.S. at close to 2 million. Of these people, 6 percent are computer analysts and programmers and another 6 percent are engineers and scientists. The rest of the workers are divided among various occupations.

But while 2 million telecommuters may sound like a large number, Adia Personnel Services of Menlo Park, California, estimates that only 7 percent of U.S. companies currently permit their employees to work at home. And of the employees who have the option to telecommute, fewer than 10 percent take advantage of the offer.

While telecommuting has been slow to catch on, many experts see the field catching fire during the 1990s. A variety of emerging social trends, as well as new state and local government regulations, are expected to give the work-at-home trend a new and stronger momentum in the years ahead.

Since home workers don't need office space, furniture or a parking spot, telecommuting can reduce these budget items.

Among other advantages, telecommuters are more likely to continue working through minor illnesses and other at-home pressures than in-house employees. This extra productivity can reflect positively on a company's bottom line. Telecommuting can also reduce the strain on a company's physical facilities. Since home workers don't need office space, furniture or a parking spot, telecommuting can reduce these budget items—if the workers come to the office only for occasional meetings.

An attractive alternative to full-fledged telecommuting is satellite "work centers." Work centers are a sort of hybrid between in-office work and pure telecommuting. By putting smaller offices in the suburbs, and linking these centers to headquarters via a WAN or internetwork, organizations can encourage workers to commute less, reducing both expenses and air pollution.

Satellite work centers are already popular in some European countries and Japan. The trend is also gaining some momentum in the

U.S. But like telecommuting in general, the concept meets resistance from managers and top executives who are accustomed to having key workers located no farther than a few footsteps away.

Network Administrators

Typically, for larger networks, a group of network support people working under a chief administrator handles certain specialized functions, such as installing and configuring network interface cards, maintaining network cabling or maintaining routers. LAN administrators for small networks are usually responsible for a broader range of network functions, including all of the above tasks.

These crucial people tend to have one of two distinct backgrounds, as discussed later in this section. The differences between them can be complementary strengths.

Large Networks

Organizations using networks that include 75 to 100 workstations usually have MIS or network support departments. Network support departments vary considerably in size, but they usually have 1 support person for every 50 to 100 users. Where support requirements are high, the number of nodes assigned to a support person is smaller.

Large support departments work best when they divide tasks into centralized and decentralized categories. The leader of the network support group should supervise all centralized tasks—those that affect the whole organization. Such tasks include capacity planning, budgeting, procurement, policy making and training procedures.

Other members of the support team handle decentralized tasks, which are narrower in scope and include network housekeeping, electronic mail, user support and specific application support.

Decentralized tasks apply only to specific networks, users or departments and not the entire corporate network.

As corporate LANs and WANs grow bigger, some kind of hierarchy of network managers tends to arise in order to function efficiently. At the lowest level there's the system manager and the LAN manager. The system manager works within a specific workgroup, worrying about such things as proper software installation on workstations and installation of interface cards. The LAN manager has the responsibility for the integrity of an individual LAN, checking local hubs, modems, local routers and monitoring network traffic. Bringing it all together is the internetwork manager, who bears the responsibility for the campus cabling plant and wide area links.

Figure 9-1
The Responsibilities of an Internetwork Manager

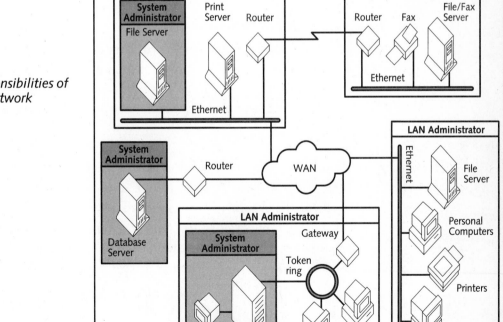

Smaller Networks

The LAN administrator for a network of fewer than 75 workstations is often the only person in the organization solely responsible for the network. He or she often combines the jobs of system manager and LAN manager, as outlined earlier. To stay on top of the job's widely varied responsibilities, the LAN administrator must educate the users, both to reduce support needs and to delegate some of the simpler network tasks.

An administrator for a smaller network needs to train a backup administrator to handle the most crucial network tasks. If the main administrator is away from the office, someone should know how to run backups, solve common problems, restart the server and perform other routine jobs.

Part-Time Administrators

Many small companies or departments don't have full-time LAN administrators. Some fairly adept person is given the job in addition to all of his or her other responsibilities. Many of these people are reluctant to accept the job; others welcome it as a chance to gain new skills.

A network with 20 stations and a file server might take 20 hours a week to administer.

Part-time administrators must have enough time to do their jobs. Inexperienced people are often not able to anticipate the support needs of a LAN. LANs with more than 20 nodes usually require a full-time administrator. To roughly estimate the amount of time required to properly administer a small LAN, start with 10 hours a week and then add a half hour per week for each workstation. This formula suggests that a network with 20 stations and a file server might take 20 hours a week to administer. The formula should be varied depending on how the network is used, but this figure is a good starting point. It is also useful in gauging the need for contract, or outsourced, network administrators.

Mainframe People and LAN People

Mainframe people (administrators with mainframe backgrounds) and LAN people (administrators with LAN-only backgrounds) have much to learn from each other. The two groups approach their jobs from different perspectives, but both bring different skills and experiences to the position.

Many new LAN functions—especially security and accounting—are modeled after existing mainframe functions.

LAN administrators with mainframe and minicomputer experience are usually formally trained in established procedures for managing computer networks and information systems. They usually have been (or still are) members of MIS or computer services departments. Many are responsible for both LANs and mainframes.

Many administrators from purely LAN backgrounds learned on the job as their organizations began networking their personal computers. They have some knowledge of mainframes, but all of their networking experience has been with LANs. Often they have had some formal training, but most of their knowledge comes from firsthand experience. These administrators face significant challenges, but they often come up with innovative, pragmatic solutions.

Mainframe People

Administrators with mainframe backgrounds usually have a lot of technical knowledge and are comfortable with a structured approach to complex tasks. When LANs are added to their systems, they sometimes discover that they must be more responsive to users; most welcome the increased human contact and appreciation.

As LAN technology evolves and LANs become more crucial to organizations, running a LAN is becoming more like running a mainframe. Many new LAN functions—especially security and accounting—are modeled after existing mainframe functions. Consequently, LAN administrators with mainframe experience can use many of the same management skills.

LAN People

Administrators from LAN-only backgrounds have a lot of experience making end users happy and more productive. The culture of personal computing is based on an independent, flexible conception of computing. Administrators from PC backgrounds may not be fully aware of the crucial need for cooperation and standardization. If the administrator doesn't provide strong leadership, the vitality and independence of PC users can lead to anarchy when a network is installed.

Many LAN administrators have no formal computer science or networking background and are often chosen because they're interested in the subject (either helping end users or working with networks). It's therefore important that these network administrators be recognized for the importance of the work that they do and that they be allowed to receive the training necessary to do their jobs well.

Working Together

As LANs become larger and more established, administrators are gradually starting to use a more systematic, mainframe-type approach while retaining the flexibility and responsiveness characteristic of LANs.

In many cases, LAN administrators work closely with mainframe people without any problems, often in related applications. LANs often are used as gateways to mainframes, providing a friendly user interface for specific mainframe applications.

Planning a LAN

Now that you know the basics of what a LAN is all about, it's time to start planning for the big move—whether it's from standalone PCs or from a mainframe—to a fully networked office environment.

Such a major changeover requires careful advance planning and budgeting. The exact details vary with each individual changeover project, but we can help you put the process in motion with some advice based on the experiences of owners and managers who have been through it.

Networking Objectives

The first step in making the changeover is to understand the needs your future LAN should fill. This isn't as easy as it sounds, since different owners and managers have different needs and networking goals. At this point, you may not even fully understand your needs. It will help to ask—and answer—the following questions.

What tasks do we need to perform on the network?

List your objectives for the networked system—do you need to keep extensive records in a database manager, build complex spreadsheets with information from several people or merely share word processing files? The tasks you list may be somewhat different from what your office currently does; for example, a networked system can give several people instant access to live database information, so more people throughout the company can have up-to-date information without requiring one person to print reports for everyone.

How does the company do those tasks now? What's wrong with (or inefficient about) how we do them now?

Is your correspondence getting lost in the filing process? If the people in your company keep spreadsheets (manual or electronic), do they need to incorporate information from other people's spreadsheets? Do desktop publishers incorporate documents that are being updated by others, right up to the last minute before they are printed?

How do we want the network to improve what we do now?

Here's where you can get creative—think about what works smoothly as well as what takes too long or is simply impossible with your present system. Some aspects of your business may not benefit from computerizing yet.

How much time do we want to spend administering the network?

LAN administration involves a variety of tasks that ensure reliable, efficient performance, and depending on the number of users, you may need to designate one or more LAN administrators. The amount of time spent administering the network depends heavily on the type of network you choose and the skills of the users. Administration is the subject of Chapter 7, and administrators are discussed earlier in this chapter.

What type of cabling makes sense for the network?

Where your employees are located can make a big difference in how to wire the network. If all of the PCs in a workgroup are close together (within the same building or on the same floor), you can choose from several types of cabling, such as twisted-pair or thin Ethernet, or ARCnet. Networks spanning longer distances or multiple buildings need to use more expensive cabling, such as thick Ethernet or fiber-optic cabling as well as bridges and routers (see Chapter 4, Cabling and Connections).

Other important considerations are data transmission speed, the ease with which you can change the network's configuration when employees move or change offices, and installation expense. Each type of network uses a particular topology, or cabling scheme—some common ones are bus, star and ring topologies. Your company's building layout can help determine which topology would be best for your situation.

Is wiring in place already?

Often, companies have existing cabling left over from previous terminal installations or unused pairs of wire in existing phone installations. These cables and wires can then be used to save on cabling costs—a major part of a network's cost. Be careful to check the quality of your wiring, however, since not all existing wire is capable of carrying a network signal. Major network vendors offer a variety of adapters that let you interconnect different types of cabling, making it easier for you to use old wiring.

What types of computers do we need to network?

Most of the popular networking products support both IBM-compatible PCs running DOS, Windows or OS/2 as well as Apple Macintoshes. However, some networking systems do not offer all of their network services to each type of client.

What problems should we watch out for once the network is installed?

Networked life is different. You're suddenly dependent on equipment that's not on your desktop. Someone has to be responsible for the shared system. The responsibilities include helping new or forgetful users, troubleshooting, backing up central files, administration of passwords and access privileges if such a system is implemented, and updating software consistently so stragglers can't disrupt the network by running old versions of a program.

Leave Room for the Future

You've probably read some computer magazine recently and no doubt been fascinated by predictions of LANs—even small business networks—supporting such advanced technologies as high-resolution video and teleconferencing. So how can you make sure that the LAN you buy today will be able to accommodate the demands of 1998 or 2010?

The answer is to think big—or at least bigger. It's always cheaper to build in extra capacity at the start than to go back and replace components at a later date. Even if your estimates project only a moderate growth in workload during the life of the network, you can still expect future technologies to place unexpected demands on your system. For proof, just ask anyone who installed a network five or six years ago, before the use of e-mail, Windows and groupware products began to soar.

Don't forget that new applications will probably require increased network bandwidth. Sound and video files transmitted in realtime require three to five times as much bandwidth as text or graphics files. Thus you'll need higher-capacity networks for multimedia applications or video conferencing.

Try to build in at least a 25 to 50 percent excess capacity in disk space, cable utilization and microprocessor speed.

When planning your LAN, try to build in at least a 25 to 50 percent excess capacity in disk space, cable utilization and microprocessor speed—even more if you're involved with a fast-growing department or company. Get an 80486 or maybe a Pentium-class machine to start with, even if your projections indicate another two years before you'll use all of its power. The added expense of providing extra capacity is insignificant compared with the cost of ripping everything up and starting over from scratch a few years down the road.

Speaking of ripping up and starting over, it's also important to remain flexible. Don't install anything that can't be replaced relatively easily. Do some serious medium-range planning, but realize that five or ten years down the road your LAN may be required to handle tasks and software not even dreamed of today.

In many respects, today's network owners face the same problem faced by superhighway builders in the 1950s. Back then, roads filled to capacity almost as soon as they were opened. Fortunately, networks are a lot more flexible than highways. With upgrades and modifications, LANs have the potential to carry enormous amounts of data. The trick lies in being able to judge your future needs and to work within the constraints of your budget and current technology.

Readying the Site

To prevent future difficulties, make sure your site has adequate electrical support.

If your organization is downsizing from a mainframe-based multiuser system, odds are your building or office can accommodate a new LAN with no extensive changes. If a LAN is your company's first venture into computer networking, you should closely evaluate your site before beginning the LAN planning or budgeting process.

Electrical support is a prime consideration. Many network products, such as servers, require substantial amounts of power and should be attached to dedicated outlets. To save costs, some electrical contractors place these devices on lower-amp circuits. To prevent future difficulties, make sure your site has adequate electrical support. Since most LAN buyers aren't electricians, it's a good idea to have an electrical expert or systems engineer do this.

Another point you'll have to consider is the physical placement of the server and other LAN hardware. An equipment room should feature adequate phone and power service with an uninterruptible power supply. It should also be in a convenient location and be secure against intrusions by unauthorized personnel. And don't forget proper airflow for cooling all this added electronic equipment! Make sure whatever closet or room you use has a new fan or duct built in for this LAN hardware.

Finally, consider the construction of your building or office. Generally speaking, older buildings present more obstacles to network installation than more modern structures. Thick plaster or concrete walls, while prized for their environmental insulation qualities, can easily double or triple cabling costs.

The Budgeting Process

LANs come in all sorts of configurations, from lower-cost peer-to-peer networks to highly sophisticated client-server LANs. You'll find there is a great deal of price flexibility within the LAN marketplace. This is lucky, because no one can plan the ideal network first and then get budget approval for it. You'll have to plan your network around a limited budget and around components that can be upgraded and expanded. You should also leave enough time to obtain all the necessary approvals and allow all the paperwork to flow through whatever channels your company requires.

Your first step toward keeping LAN costs under control is to discuss the project with a financial expert who can help you get a handle on potential expenses.

Use an Auditor

The price of networking a business or office can quickly skyrocket unless you keep a sharp eye on the bottom line. Your first step toward keeping LAN costs under control is to discuss the project with a financial expert who can help you get a handle on potential expenses.

An auditor—either a company financial officer or an outside budgeting expert—can identify hidden costs you probably never even considered. For example, a good auditor will force you to break down expenses for every item in detail. Such work, though it isn't pleasant, is the only way to get an accurate view of what it will cost to install and maintain your network. It can also help you separate vital products and services from expensive doodads.

The perfect LAN supports an unlimited number of users and peripherals and still provides good response time, but in the real world, trade-offs must be made between cost, size and performance. You must decide in advance just how much performance and size you're willing to sacrifice for savings.

There's no simple solution or shortcut when it comes to resolving this problem. All you can do is study vendor specifications, talk to as many knowledgeable people as you can and make the necessary decisions on the basis of your own best judgment.

The Cost of Support and Maintenance

Over time, support expenses can actually outstrip the expense of a LAN's hardware, software and installation.

Over time, support expenses can actually outstrip the expense of a LAN's hardware, software and installation. So in addition to the initial cost of the equipment, you should estimate the continuing costs of the network system. Include such items as printer supplies, cabling and installation costs (for new users or those relocating their desks) and service contracts or repair costs.

Be sure to provide for the costs of training your users. In some cases, this might only include familiarizing them with the new capabilities that the network offers them, such as shared files and printers. In other cases, training might include classes on new networked applications unlike anything they've used before.

Also, don't forget to provide for the costs of upgrading software. Older versions of some software might not work on a network, and you may also want to use the networking features found in new versions of existing programs. And while you're planning your network, you may choose to bring your users up to a common hardware base (if you're switching everyone to Windows, for instance), so you may have to include costs for upgrading the personal computers by adding more memory or better monitors. In the case of mainframe users, these costs will generally be lower with a LAN, but they still must be taken into consideration.

Other Costs

The costs of protecting your LAN against data leaks shouldn't be overlooked. While data encryption and password schemes are relatively inexpensive, protecting your hardware against physical break-ins can run into big bucks.

Be sure to ask your auditor about the tax implications of LAN equipment depreciation.

Be sure to ask your auditor about the tax implications of LAN equipment depreciation. This is an area in which the services of a financial expert can really pay off.

Installing LAN cabling is a labor-intensive job. To minimize office disruption, most managers want the work done in a hurry. But be certain you understand local work rules and labor union requirements before establishing a timetable for completion. Also include the cost of space for equipment and other LAN-related products in your budget. Your financial advisor will put a price tag on these costs, so you should, too.

Finally, consider the money to be made from getting rid of your mainframe. Used computer brokers will pay to take your old hardware off your hands, but be realistic when including these sums in your budget. After all, "old iron" doesn't command the prices it used to, although the gear will bring you more cash today than it will tomorrow.

Approval

Most likely, the go-ahead for your LAN will have to come from higher-ups. To make sure that you leave enough time for all approvals, write down a list of all the people who will have to approve your plans, estimating the time each step will take.

Lastly, you may need to justify the costs of the LAN and be able to measure its effectiveness. To do that, you can choose a financial criterion for gauging the success of the reduction in data-entry costs, improvement in customer response time, increased sales for the computerized department or any other measure appropriate to your business.

No business owner or manager wants to be associated with massive cost overruns. So do your homework up front to make sure your LAN project doesn't become a minefield of unpleasant surprises. The possible rewards of the right LAN are too great to do otherwise.

10 / Buyer's Guide

....

There is no such thing as a complete buyer's guide to network-related hardware and software. No wonder, since there's almost no limit to what is "network-related." A really comprehensive buyer's guide would include every brand and model of personal computer, every software package on the market (after all, if it runs on a computer connected to a network, it's part of the story) and every network widget and gadget you can think of. This would be impossible for even the largest book, since product details change daily.

Therefore, the goal of this chapter is not to be all-inclusive, but rather to give you passing familiarity with some of the industry's most significant or best-selling products, listed in a straightforward directory format.

If you haven't already read Chapters 2, 3 and 5, make sure to refer back to these for explanations of the product categories. Because vendor offerings change so frequently, a *general* understanding of networking product types will be more useful than specific names or numbers. Similarly, because of the volatility of pricing, we have left prices out, but recommend that you call the manufacturers (phone numbers are listed here) to get the most current information.

Accounting

Computer Associates

CA Accpac Plus
CA Accpac Plus runs on DOS, OS/2 and Macintosh clients. Available modules include general ledger, accounts receivable, accounts payable, purchase requisition, order entry, purchase order, job costing, inventory, payroll, cash management, retail invoicing and Dyna-View Windowing System Manager.
(800) 225-5224

DacEasy Inc.

DacEasy Network Accounting
This offers general ledger, accounts receivable, accounts payable, purchase order, inventory, payroll and cash management modules.
(214) 248-0305

Great Plains Software

Great Plains Accounting
Great Plains Accounting runs on DOS, Macintosh, Unix and Windows clients. Modules include general ledger, accounts receivable, accounts payable, purchase requisition, order entry, purchase order, job costing, inventory, payroll and cash management.
(800) 456-0025

Macola

Macola Accounting Software

This program can run on DOS, Windows, OS/2 and Unix clients. Modules include general ledger, accounts receivable, accounts payable, purchase requisition, order entry, purchase order, job costing, inventory, payroll, assets and depreciation, material requirements planning and shop floor control.
(800) 468-0834

Platinum Desktop Software

Platinum

This program runs on DOS clients over NetBIOS and NetWare. Modules include general ledger, accounts receivable, accounts payable, purchase requisition, order entry, purchase order, job costing, inventory and payroll.
(714) 727-1250

Platinum Desktop Software

SeQuel to Platinum

This is a client-server accounting program for Windows NT. It includes general ledger, accounts payable, accounts receivable and a financial report generator.
(714) 727-1250

RealWorld

RealWorld Accounting

RealWorld Accounting and Business Software runs on DOS clients. It offers modules for general ledger, accounts receivable, accounts payable, purchase requisition, order entry, purchase order, job costing, inventory, payroll and cash management.
(800) 678-6336 or (603) 224-2200

RealWorld

RealWorld Spectrum Accounting

This Windows-based accounting package is aimed at small businesses, combining accounts receivable, sales invoicing, inventory management, accounts payable, general ledger, payroll and check reconciliation into one integrated package.

(800) 678-6336 or (603) 224-2200

SourceMate Information Systems

AccountMate Premiere

This is a multiuser accounting system based on the DOS version of Microsoft's *FoxPro*. It offers features such as pull-down menus plus selectable password protection for individual modules and functions within them. Source code is also available.

(415) 381-1011

Backup Software

Cheyenne Software

ARCserve

ARCserve is a leading server-based, enterprise-wide backup program for NetWare. With the NetWare versions of *Btrieve*, SQL and *Oracle Server*, *ARCServe* can back up a whole online database *including* transactions that occur during backups.

(800) 243-9462 or (516) 484-5110

Emerald Systems

Xpress Librarian

Xpress Librarian is a workstation-based backup program that allows NetWare servers and local hard drives to be backed up to tape. It features a Windows interface.

(800) 767-2587 or (619) 673-2161

Intel
StorageExpress
Intel's StorageExpress system is an integrated, multiserver tape backup system with its own dedicated CPU, SCSI and Ethernet interfaces. Connected directly to two 8mm tape drives, the Storage-Express processor runs NetWare runtime and a tape-server NLM. The Windows-based management interface—run from an administrator's workstation—can do everything right down to printing tape labels.
(800) 538-3373

Database Software

askSam Systems
askSam for Windows
askSam for Windows is a product intended for managing large amounts of text. It includes database, text-retrieval and word processing modules.
(800) 800-1997

Borland
dBASE IV Version 2.0
This venerable database product now lets you incorporate a mouse into the user interface of programs you write, and it has been increased in speed substantially.
(800) 331-0877 or (408) 438-8400

Borland
Paradox for DOS, Paradox for Windows
Paradox for DOS is a fast, proven database program that can link to SQL databases using the optional *Paradox SQL Link* product. *Paradox for Windows* is an advanced database that can act as an OLE

client and fully supports DDE. It has a graphical, object-oriented programming environment.
(800) 331-0877 or (408) 438-8400

ClearAccess

ClearAccess

This is a SQL query and report front end that's available for Windows or the Macintosh. Queries can be stored for reuse via script recording.
(800) 522-4252 or (515) 472-7077

DataEase International

DataEase

This DOS-based database product offers a menu-driven interface, LAN record locking and Query By Example capabilities. An optional add-in, *DataEase SQL Connect*, lets you develop applications that work with external database servers.
(800) 243-5123 or (203) 374-8000

Edify

Edify Information Agent

This program is a query tool and report writer that works with Oracle, Informix and host databases. An intelligent-agent-based system, it automates retrieval, manipulation and delivery of information across networks.
(800) 944-0056 or (408) 982-2000

Gupta Technologies

Quest

Quest is a query tool and report writer that lets users create, edit and browse SQL tables, issue queries and build WYSIWYG reports from corporate databases without any knowledge of SQL.
(800) 388-4550 or (415) 321-9500

Gupta Technologies

SQL Network

SQL Network is an add-on that makes all popular SQL databases—
on mainframes, minis and PC networks—accessible to NetWare
PC applications.
(800) 388-4550 or (415) 321-9500

Gupta Technologies

SQLBase Server

Gupta's *SQLBase Server* is a high-performance product that comes
in versions for DOS, OS/2, NetWare and Unix servers. It can compress messages sent between client and server, making it suitable for
information-rich image databases.
(800) 876-3267 or (415) 321-9500

Gupta Technologies

SQLWindows

SQLWindows lets developers create graphical SQL database applications that run under Windows and OS/2 Presentation Manager. It
provides access to SQL database servers running on PCs, PC
LANs, minicomputers and mainframes.
(800) 388-4550 or (415) 321-9500

IBM

Extended Services with Database Server for OS/2

IBM's *Extended Services* features SQL syntax closely matching DB2
(one of the company's database products for larger systems). An
optional package lets users connect transparently to DB2 mainframe databases. Another feature of the product is its support for
the Database Application Remote Interface, which lets programmers move portions of client applications to the server via Dynamic
Link Libraries.
(800) 426-2255 or (914) 765-1900

Information Builders
PC/Focus
PC/Focus runs on DOS and OS/2 clients, supporting client-server architecture via ANSI-standard SQL.
(310) 615-0735

Informix
INFORMIX ONLine for NetWare
INFORMIX ONLine for NetWare is a version of the company's SQL-based data manager, currently the most popular in the Unix environment. It supports client-server architecture, ANSI SQL and an unlimited number of tables and records.
(800) 438-7627 or (913) 599-7100

Microrim
R:Base
R:Base 4.0 runs in 32-bit protected mode in either DOS or OS/2 versions. It supports Query By Example and uses SQL as its language for data manipulation.
(800) 628-6990 or (206) 649-9500

Microsoft
Access
More for the knowledgeable end user than the database programmer seeking to write turnkey systems, *Access* can read and join tables from *Btrieve*, *dBASE*, *Paradox* 3.5 and *SQL Server.* It also features click-and-drag report formatting.
(800) 426-9400 or (206) 882-8080

Microsoft
FoxPro for DOS and *FoxPro for Windows*
Known as one of the fastest xBASE-compatible databases, *FoxPro* now comes in DOS and Windows versions. In Version 2.5, a new

algorithm reduces network traffic by determining the minimum information necessary to read from the server at any given moment. (800) 426-9400 or (206) 882-8080

Microsoft
Microsoft SQL Server 4.2
SQL Server 4.2 is an OS/2-based version of Sybase *SQL Server*. It offers fault tolerance, mirroring and the ability to back up to tape even while a database is live. It supports a wide variety of clients. (800) 426-9400 or (206) 882-8080

Novell
NetWare SQL
It has a low marketing profile, but *NetWare SQL* is a good choice for NetWare users. Tightly integrated into the NetWare file system, this 32-bit Netware Loadable Module gets the most out of the underlying hardware. Supports Mac, DOS, OS/2 and Windows clients.
(800) 773-9673

Object Design
ObjectStore
This is an object-oriented database manager that runs on DOS, Unix and Windows clients. It supports a client-server architecture. (800) 962-9620 or (617) 270-9797

Oracle
Oracle Server for NetWare
This database management product has been ported to more than 100 platforms. Cross-platform support lets users simultaneously access data tables stored on different server platforms.
(800) 542-1170

Pilot Software Inc.

Lightship

This Windows product can combine graphics with information pulled in for SQL databases. Best suited to creating executive information systems, it does allow users to modify data.
(800) 944-0094

PowerSoft

PowerBuilder

PowerBuilder is an applications development environment that supports most SQL products but also has its own database manager. It's ideal for creating graphical, client-server database applications because its object-oriented methods lessen the need to write your own SQL code.
(800) 395-3525

Revelation Technologies

OpenEngine and *Advanced Revelation*

These databases, for DOS, OS/2 or Unix, support file-server architecture and ANSI SQL.
(800) 262-4747

Software Publishing Corporation

Superbase

A Windows-based product, *Superbase* permits you to create sophisticated applications without a single line of programming. It runs on any network that supports Windows and it uses built-in file- and record-locking schemes that do not rely on programming or on the network itself.
(800) 336-8360

Sybase

SQL Server for NetWare

SQL Server for NetWare is the NetWare Loadable Module-based version of the basic Sybase product. Though not inexpensive, it's one of the fastest SQL databases available for PCs.
(800) 879-2273

TECHgnosis

SequeLink

SequeLink is a type of product *LAN Magazine* has termed "client-server middleware." It provides direct, transparent access to micro, mainframe or minicomputer SQL databases from within Windows, Macintosh, Unix, OS/2 and VMS applications.
(407) 997-6687

Trinzic Corporation

Forest and Trees

This is an analytical tool for viewing SQL data (and data in most common PC file formats) within Windows. It doesn't allow users to modify data, but it's ideal for executive information systems.
(603) 427-0444

E-Mail and Groupware

1Soft

Above and Beyond for Windows

This program concentrates on time management for individuals or groups. It offers "drag-and-drop" scheduling and a meeting-maker feature that finds blocks of free time that are common to all.
(800) 326-4391

Alisa Systems

AlisaMail

AlisaMail runs on DOS, Macintosh and VAX clients on AppleShare and DECnet networks. It supports graphic file attachments and offers gateways to other e-mail programs (such as *All-in-1* and *VMS-mail*).
(800) 628-3274

Beyond

BeyondMail

For Novell networks, *BeyondMail* is an e-mail program with a rule-based scripting language. Users can develop forms that prompt the recipient to fill in various fields, then send replies accordingly. It comes with form templates for phone messages, meeting requests and customer support.
(800) 845-8511 or (617) 621-0095

CE Software

QuickMail

QuickMail is a Macintosh e-mail program that runs on any Apple-Share-compatible file server. A wide variety of gateways is offered for linking to PCs and mainframes.
(515) 224-1995

Chronos Software

Enterprise

This LAN version of *Who-What-When* includes personal scheduling, group and resource scheduling, time management and an address database.
(415) 920-6900

Computer Associates

CA-SuperProject

CA-SuperProject runs on DOS, Windows and VAX clients. It supports interdependent concurrent projects, Gantt and PERT charts and up to 255 users.

(800) 225-5224

Computer Associates

CA-UpToDate

CA-UpToDate is a Windows-only package that offers a color-coded approach to group scheduling. Its default interface is via a Gantt chart.

(800) 225-5224

Da Vinci Systems

The Coordinator

The Coordinator comes with an integrated calendar for group scheduling. It also brings structure to e-mail dialogues by using formatted conversation types: Note, Inform, Question, Offer, Request, Agree or What If.

(800) 328-4624

Elan Software

Goldmine

Goldmine runs on DOS and Windows clients, offering integrated e-mail, scheduling plus workflow automation. It maintains a calendar, historical records and other information on clients. It also tracks sales forecasts and can produce reports.

(800) 654-3526

Enable Software
Higgins
Available in DOS or OS/2 versions, *Higgins* combines its own e-mail system, a personal calendar plus group and resource scheduling.
(800) 888-0684

Folio Software
MailBag
This e-mail add-on product is designed to store an archive of messages that can be retrieved quickly when needed. It automatically indexes and compresses e-mail into its database, then lets you access old messages via keywords or a full-text search.
(800) 543-6546 or (801) 375-3700

Futurus
Futurus Team
Futurus Team includes e-mail, workgroup scheduling and to-do listing. It comes with client software for both Windows and DOS.
(800) 327-8296 or (404) 392-7979

IBM
Current-OfficeVision/VM
This workgroup version of *Current* is intended for those who connect to a mainframe from a Windows PC.
(800) 426-2255

IBM
Time and Place/2
Time and Place/2 is a group scheduler for OS/2 that works with the IBM Extended Services Database Manager. It allows either OS/2 or

Windows clients cooperatively to schedule events, to-do lists, conference rooms and more.
(800) 426-2255

Keyfile
Keyfile
Keyfile is an image-centered groupware product that distributes graphical images of data files. An administrator can define steps that must be taken before a document is passed to the next participant. *Keyfile* includes drivers for typical scanning and printing peripherals, including Okidata's DOC.IT.
(603) 883-3800

Lotus Development
cc:Mail
This e-mail program runs on DOS, Windows, OS/2, Mac or Unix clients and links via macros to other Lotus applications (such as *1-2-3*, *AmiPro* and *Notes*). Versions are also available for palmtop portables such as Hewlett-Packard's 100LX. Gateways to a wide variety of other systems are offered, including PROFS, *All-in-1*, SMTP, X.400, SNADS, VMS, Sprint, MCI and SoftSwitch.
(800) 448-2500

Lotus Development
1-2-3 Release 4.0
This Windows version of Lotus comes in a single version that can be used in standalone or network mode. Mail-enabled, it has a feature called Version Manager. This allows users to create and manage different versions of worksheets while also sharing them with others. Who is permitted to make changes is controlled by a "rights token" passed around the network.
(800) 343-5414

Lotus Development

Lotus Notes

Much more than an e-mail package, *Lotus Notes* is actually a client-server database whose purpose is message transfer. It can be used to develop a series of messages into a logically structured conference. *Notes* also has hooks into other Lotus applications, such as *1-2-3* (for which it intelligently manages worksheet versions).
(800) 346-1305

Microsoft

Microsoft Mail

Microsoft Mail lets users send or receive anything in their messages—pictures, charts, graphs, spreadsheets. A "message finder" feature helps those with large volumes of incoming mail, scanning for key words.
(800) 624-9400

Microsoft

Microsoft Schedule Plus

This Windows product works in conjunction with *Microsoft Mail*, meaning that administrators do not need to spend any time creating a user list. Its "Auto-pick" feature automatically suggests times for group meetings.
(800) 624-9400

Microsystems Software Inc.

CaLANdar

Available for both Windows and DOS, *CaLANdar* is a group scheduling program that works independently of your e-mail program. It makes it easy to schedule meetings and resources. *CaLANdar* can generate printed calendars for most popular daytimers, and it also has built-in support for the Sharp Wizard.
(508) 879-9000

Optika Imaging Systems

FilePower

FilePower for DOS and Windows clients routes, stores and retrieves images throughout a company. It can use SQL Server, SQLBase and other file servers.

(719) 548-9800

PC DOCS

PC DOCS

PC DOCS (Document Organization and Control System) is a NetWare Loadable Module that tracks documents by attributes such as author, typist, subject, project and more. It can automatically name files and launch applications that created them.

(800) 933-3627 or (904) 942-3627

PowerCore

Network Scheduler 3

This group scheduling program features DOS and Windows client interfaces that are remarkably similar. With links to the HP 95LX and Sharp Wizard, it allows rescheduling meetings via a simple cut-and-paste operation.

(800) 237-4754 or (815) 468-3737

Primavera

Primavera Project Planner

This program supports interdependent concurrent projects, Gantt and PERT charts and unlimited users.

(800) 423-0245 or (215) 667-8600

Reach Software

MailMAN

In versions for NetWare MHS or Banyan VINES, *MailMAN* is an easy-to-install mail program. Especially strong in management

functions, it features a folder-based desktop that makes it simple to read, forward, reply to or delete messages *en masse*.
(800) MAILFLO (624-5356) or (408) 733-8685

Richmond Technologies
Maximizer
Built around Novell's *Btrieve* database engine, *Maximizer* is tailored for storing company addresses and sales contact information.
(604) 299-2121

Saros
Mezzanine
Mezzanine runs on most local area networks, tracking documents by author, typist, file name, subject and more.
(206) 646-1066

SoftSolutions Technology
SoftSolutions
SoftSolutions is a document-tracking system available in both DOS and Windows versions. It lets users trace documents using attributes such as author, typist, file name, subject, project, document type or originating application.
(801) 226-6000

SuperTime
SuperTime
This Canadian company offers an integrated appointment scheduler, contact directory with call list, e-mail with message center, task manager and reference libraries. Its database supports a file-server architecture.
(416) 764-3530

Symantec
ACT! Network
ACT! Network manages both contact and calendar information. It provides record locking, password protection and private databases.
(800) 441-7234

ViewStar
ViewStar
ViewStar routes and retrieves images for DOS, Windows or OS/2 clients using *SQL Server, Oracle* and Sybase.
(510) 652-7827

Wang Labs
Integrated Image Systems for Windows
This PC-based product uses a proprietary back end to route, store and retrieve images. Wang also produces several other client-server image management solutions, including *Open/Image* and *Seaview.*
(800) 639-9264 or (508) 459-5000

WordPerfect
WordPerfect Office
WordPerfect Office is intended for those who have standardized on WordPerfect. It's an e-mail and group resource-scheduling product that has a WordPerfect-like user interface. Version 4.0, recently released, offers DOS, Windows and Macintosh clients (Unix is planned). It offers rule-based e-mail filtering and the unusual ability to retrieve e-mail messages before the recipient has read them. A "routing slip" feature lets you move information from user to user in predetermined order.
(800) 451-5151 or (801) 225-5000

Network Interface Cards

3Com
EtherLink/NB
This is a 32-bit NuBus card for connecting Macintosh II systems to Ethernet LANs.
(800) NET-3COM (638-3266)

3Com
EtherLink III and EtherLink 16 TP
Available in ISA, Micro Channel or EISA versions, 3Com's Ether-Link III features support for twisted-pair and thin or thick coax, all on one board. A "pipelining" design makes it one of the fastest adapters on the market. The EtherLink 16 TP is designed to connect with hubs that were manufactured before the 10BASE-T specifications were standardized.
(800) NET-3COM (638-3266)

Accton Technology
EtherPocket and RingPocket
Accton's parallel-port adapters have been acclaimed for their speed and relatively low pricing.
(800) 926-9288 or Fast Fax info (510) 226-8875

Asante
AsanteLite and MacCon+
Asante produces Ethernet cards for most Macintosh models. The MacCon+ cards include SNMP (Simple Network Management Protocol) agents and a five-year warranty; the AsanteLite cards come with simplified packaging and without SNMP support.
(800) 662-9686 or (408) 435-8388

Asante

Mini EN/SC

Asante's Mini EN/SC is a SCSI-to-Ethernet connector for Apple PowerBooks and other Macintoshes without available slots. It comes with connecting cables for both PowerBooks and desktops.
(800) 662-9686 or (408) 435-8388

CNet

CN600E and CN911E

The CN600E is a 16-bit client Ethernet adapter compatible with the Eagle NE2000 and software configurable. The CN911E is a bus-mastering EISA adapter configurable via software and intended for servers.
(800) 486-2638 or (408) 954-8000

Eagle

NE2000, NE2000 Plus and NE3200

Originally sold by Novell, the 16-bit NE2000 is the client Ethernet adapter by which all competitors are judged. The NE2000 Plus is a newer, software-configurable version. Eagle's NE3200 is the EISA version for servers.
(800) 733-2453 or (408) 441-7453

Gateway Communications

G/Ethernet and G/EtherTwist adapters

Gateway Communications produces a wide range of Ethernet adapters for Apple PDS, NuBus, ISA, EISA and Micro Channel machines.
(800) 367-6555 or (714) 553-1555

Hewlett-Packard
EtherTwist

HP produces Ethernet cards for 10BASE-T LANs using EISA, ISA or Micro Channel. Its HP 27247B is one of the highest-performing ISA client adapters, suitable even for servers on small networks.
(800) 752-0900 or Fast Fax info (800) 333-1917

Intel
EtherExpress 16C, EtherExpress FlashC, TokenExpress ISA/16 and EtherExpress 32

Intel's Express adapters feature switchless installation and automatic IRQ and I/O selection. The EtherExpress FlashC card allows administrators to store PC asset information in its flash memory. The EtherExpress 32 has been hailed as one of the fastest 32-bit EISA cards for servers, partly due to its fast static RAM.
(800) 538-3373

Kingston
EtherRx cards

With a list price about $50 lower than many competitors, Kingston's EtherRx interface cards claim to be faster and require less utilization of a host CPU. The company also produces a 10BASE-T concentrator.
(800) 435-2620 or (714) 435-2600

Microdyne
NE2000, NE2000 Plus, NTR2000

Microdyne offers a range of Ethernet and token-ring adapters co-developed with Novell.
(800) 255-3967

Pure Data

In addition to an array of ISA or Micro Channel cards for ARCnet and Ethernet, Pure Data produces network interface cards for the proprietary slots on many Toshiba laptops.
(416) 731-6444

Standard Microsystems Corporation

Standard Microsystems produces a wide variety of low-cost NICs, including token ring and Ethernet adapters. Its EtherCard Plus Elite 32T is an EISA card with dual Ethernet controllers and dual RJ-45 connectors, making it a good choice for EISA desktops that have been pressed into server use.
(800) 762-4968

Thomas-Conrad

Thomas-Conrad offers a wide variety of Ethernet and token-ring interface cards. Its entry-level product is the TC5143, a switchless, software-configurable NIC for all Ethernet types. It offers four diagnostic LEDs and a socket for an optional boot ROM.
(800) 332-8683

Tiara

EtherExcel
Tiara's EtherExcel is a card that is software-configurable and has a boot ROM socket for diskless workstations. It connects to either coaxial or twisted-pair cabling.
(800) 638-4272 or (415) 965-1700

Tiara

Ethernet Universal LANCard
This is a 16-bit adapter intended for both clients and servers.
(800) 638-4272 or (415) 965-1700

Xircom

Pocket and Credit Card Adapters

Xircom, which pioneered the idea of an external LAN adapter that connects to a portable's parallel port, now offers these along with PCMCIA credit card-sized adapters. Its latest external adapters have shrunk considerably, and now draw all the power they need from a portable's keyboard or mouse port—no AC adapter is required.
(800) GET-4LAN (438-4526)

Network Operating Systems

Apple

AppleShare Pro 1.0

Introduced with the Workgroup Server 95, AppleShare Pro runs on top of A/UX, Apple's version of Unix. It can now support as many as 200 concurrently connected users and 5,000 open files.
(800) 776-2333 or (408) 996-1010

Artisoft

LANtastic

The most popular peer-to-peer NOS, LANtastic allows sharing files, printers and CD-ROM drives. It also supports modem-sharing products that use NetBIOS. Remote access is possible via an optional package, Articom, as are Macintosh and NetWare connections.
(800) 846-9726 or (602) 293-4000

Banyan

ENS for NetWare

ENS is a product that brings Banyan's StreetTalk to NetWare servers. A dedicated ENS server monitors about 15 other NetWare

servers, propagating new users and other changes from machine to machine. Besides simplifying NetWare management, ENS acts as a way to easily join VINES and NetWare networks.
(800) 828-2404 or (508) 898-1000

Banyan
VINES 5.5
Banyan's VINES (VIrtual NEtwork Operating System) is popular among companies with large, multiserver networks. It runs on top of Unix—either Banyan's own version or SCO Unix (though the NFS protocol is not supported). VINES simplifies accessing resources on any server without special batch files or logon scripts. The StreetTalk database held at every server records the name, location and attributes of every user and resource worldwide (servers automatically pass StreetTalk updates among themselves). A directory assistance function then lets users search for resources. DOS, Windows, Macintosh and OS/2 clients are all supported.
(800) 222-6926 or (508) 898-1000

Hayes
LANStep
LANStep is a low-cost software package that permits building a peer-to-peer LAN using any manufacturer's Ethernet cards. Can connect to NetWare or TCP/IP LANs.
(404) 840-9200

IBM
OS/2 LAN Server 3.0
Somewhat overlooked in the marketplace, IBM's OS/2 LAN Server is a capable NOS with disk fault tolerance, UPS support and the ability to boot either DOS or OS/2 from the server. It also allows administrators to define a one-word alias for any resource on the network. Since LAN Server runs on top of OS/2 2.0, it is possible

for a server to act as a workstation also, if need be. DOS, Windows, OS/2 and Unix clients are all supported.

(800) 426-4255 or (914) 765-1900

Microsoft

LAN Manager 2.2

Microsoft's older NOS, LAN Manager 2.2 runs on top of OS/2 1.3 and is set to be replaced by Windows NT. However, it remains a versatile operating system, with support for a wide variety of clients (DOS, OS/2, Mac, Windows for Workgroups, etc.) and transport protocols. However, Unix users won't be able to mount LAN Manager 2.2 volumes.

(800) 426-9400 or (206) 882-8080

Microsoft

Windows for Workgroups

Tightly integrated with Windows, this peer-to-peer LAN permits file, printer and CD-ROM sharing. PCs running only DOS can act as clients, but not servers. Windows for Workgroups users can also connect to NetWare or LAN Manager servers.

(800) 426-9400 or (206) 882-8080

Microsoft

Windows NT

This is a 32-bit version of Windows featuring support for preemptive multitasking and symmetrical multiprocessing. All Windows NT workstations can act as servers; however, Microsoft also offers LAN Manager for Windows NT, which helps manage "domains" of multiple servers. LAN Manager for Windows NT will also support advanced fault-tolerance features, including disk mirroring, drive duplexing, striping and uninterruptible power supplies.

(800) 426-9400 or (206) 882-8080

Novell

NetWare 3.11

For several years the corporate standard, Novell NetWare 3.11 is efficiently written and runs well on even 386 servers. NetWare Loadable Modules (NLMs) let you customize a server for various needs, including simultaneous support for DOS, OS/2, Mac and Unix clients. Versions of NetWare that run on top of VMS and Unix are also available. The NetWare Names Service option permits copying lists of users and resources from server to server (in a fashion similar to, although less complete than, VINES' Street-Talk).

(800) 638-9273

Novell

NetWare 4.01

NetWare 4.01 includes the functions of previous NetWare versions and adds a naming service that globally positions each user and resource in the network (so each user logs in only once, no matter how many resources they use). All servers know the rights of all users. Also included is advanced Windows support, active security auditing and data compression.

(800) 638-9273

Novell

NetWare Lite

NetWare Lite is a DOS-based peer-to-peer package that integrates easily with existing NetWare servers. It even has a NetWare 4.0-like feature that allows a user to log on to multiple servers by giving just one command. E-mail is not included, but almost any third-party package may be used.

(800) 453-1267 or (801) 429-7000

Novell

Unixware

Unixware is a version of Unix System V, Release 4, for Intel-based PCs. It has a graphical user interface built on the Open Software Foundation's Motif, can execute DOS or Windows programs and allows connecting to any NetWare servers (not just those running the NFS NLM).
(800) 486-4835

Performance Technology

POWERLan

Interoperable with Windows for Workgroups, POWERLan allows DOS-based PCs to share resources with those also running Windows. Remote screen sharing is built in, with modem access being an option.
(800) 327-8526 or (210) 349-2000

Tiara Systems

10NET

By spreading itself throughout upper memory, 10NET can load on a 386 or 486 system while using almost no conventional memory. Unlike many similar packages, 10NET also includes disk threshold monitoring, so administrators can set limits on the amount of disk space users take up.
(800) 638-4272 or (415) 965-1700

Print Servers

Artisoft

Central Station

Intended to connect several different portable PCs to a network, the Central Station has two serial ports, two parallel ports plus an

Ethernet connection. It can also be set up as a print server with Artisoft's NetWare Print Server Stationware program (included).
(800) 846-9726 or (602) 293-4000

ASP Computer Products
JetLAN/P200
The JetLAN/P200 connects parallel printers directly to an Ethernet network. It offers the option of setting up the print server as either a dedicated server (Novell PSERVER mode) or a remote print server (NetWare RPRINTER mode). Unlike some similar units, it also includes a metal case plus LED status indicators to monitor hub and server connections.
(408) 746-2965

Castelle
LANpress and JetPress
Castelle's LANpress is an economical external device that connects up to four printers via one Ethernet or token ring connection. The JetPress connects a single LaserJet printer via its I/O slot.
(800) 289-7555

Eagle
NPE 400
The NPE is a print server that attaches to the parallel port on any printer. It can be installed as either a dedicated server (PSERVER mode) or remote print server (RPRINTER mode). It supports PCL and PostScript and can download fonts from workstation to printer automatically when a user first logs in. Unlike some similar devices, the NPE 400 also prints "banner pages" between jobs.
(800) 733-2453 or (408) 441-7453

Extended Systems Inc.

ExtendNet and Pocket Print Server

Extended Systems Inc. produces a wide variety of internal cards for connecting Hewlett-Packard LaserJets directly to Ethernet or token ring networks. Some models provide automatic PCL/PostScript switching or multiple-protocol support. The Pocket Print Server, on the other hand, is an external device that works through the parallel port of other laser printers.

(800) 235-7576

Hewlett-Packard

JetDirect

HP's JetDirect cards permit connecting LaserJet or DeskJet printers directly to a network. Models are available to support LocalTalk, Ethernet or token ring in most environments.

(800) 752-0900 or Fast Fax info (800) 333-1917

Intel

LANSpool for NetWare

Intel's LANSpool for NetWare is a software print server that, like many similar programs, runs on a dedicated or nondedicated workstation. The difference here is that *LANSpool for FAX* software is also included.

(800) 538-3373 or (503) 629-7354

Intel

NetPort II

NetPort II provides two parallel ports and one serial port for printer connections (though only two ports may be active simultaneously).

(800) 538-3373 or (503) 629-7354

Xircom

PEPS-10BT

PEPS-10BT is a pocket-size external adapter for twisted-pair Ethernet. It lets any parallel printer act as a dedicated print server, though it does not provide peer-to-peer access (e.g., it cannot be used when a network file server is not also operational).

(818) 878-7600

Printers

Compaq

PageMarq 15 and PageMarq 20

Rated at either 15 or 20 pages per minute, Compaq's PageMarq printers feature both Adobe PostScript Level 2 and PCL 5. Paper-handling capacity of the PageMarq 20 is 1,500 sheets. Both models feature an Ethernet interface option with a Novell-compatible administrator utility.

(713) 370-0670

Gemicom

7170

Based on a Toshiba print engine, this 17-ppm printer comes with two 250-sheet input trays and a 500-page output tray. It stacks on top of optional 1,500-sheet input and output bins. A ten-bin collator is another option. PostScript is optional, as are NetWare interfaces for 10BASE-T or token ring.

(800) 443-6426 or (703) 949-1000

Hewlett-Packard

LaserJet 4Si and 4Si MX

HP's LaserJet 4Si comes with a 17-ppm print engine, a 25MHz Intel RISC processor and two 500-sheet paper trays. It also offers a

Bi-Tronics parallel interface (for two-way communication with the host computer) and resolution-enhanced 600 dpi output. Options include JetDirect network interfaces, a power envelope feeder, a print duplexer and a 2,000-sheet output stacker. The 4Si MX comes with PostScript, Ethernet and AppleTalk interfaces and automatic language switching. It supports up to ten different network operating systems, switching between protocols on the fly.
(800) 752-0900 or (208) 323-2551

IBM by Lexmark
LaserPrinter 4039 16L
This printer comes with a 16-ppm engine, PostScript Level 1 and a 500-sheet input drawer. Also included are 52 resident fonts and 4MB of RAM. Supporting LAN Manager, NetWare, LAN Server and AIX networks, it switches automatically between the parallel or serial ports and optional network interface cards.
(800) 358-5835 or (606) 232-3000

Output Technology Corp.
LaserMatrix 1000
Running at 16 pages per minute, the LaserMatrix 1000 is unusual in having a tractor-feed mechanism instead of a sheet feeder. This lets it handle forms and card stock up to 20 pounds. It also features Microsoft's TrueImage PostScript-compatible interpreter. A network interface is an option from Extended Systems.
(509) 536-0468

QMS
PS-1700
The PS-1700 uses the same Canon NX print engine as the HP LaserJet IIISi, with two 500-sheet input trays and a 500-sheet output tray. Its Intel 80960 RISC processor and 8MB of RAM provide fast

PostScript printing; you can attach internal or external SCSI hard disks for font storage. A variety of network interface cards is available. (800) 523-2696

Texas Instruments

microLaser XL Turbo PS 35

TI's microLaser XL is a 16-ppm printer for small workgroups, supporting workloads of up to 25,000 pages per month. Its 16MHz Weitek RISC controller provides rapid PostScript Level 2 printing. Only a parallel port is standard, but you can add Ethernet via a board from Printer Systems Corporation. (800) 527-3500

Remote Access

Cayman

GatorLink

The GatorLink is a three-port server that allows up to three Macs to dial into an AppleTalk/Ethernet network remotely. (800) 473-4776

DCA

Remote LAN Node

DCA's *Remote LAN Node* is a software solution that provides remote access to NetWare (IPX) or Unix (IP) hosts. (800) 348-3221 or (404) 442-4000

Gateway Communications

LAN Expander

LAN Expander is a versatile hardware/software product that allows three different types of remote access to a NetWare network: Re-

mote NetWare access mode, Remote Keyboard and Screen Mode, and PC Remote Control mode.
(800) 367-6555 or (714) 553-1555

Shiva
LanRover
Shiva's LanRover comes in versions dedicated to NetWare, Apple-Talk (either Ethernet or LocalTalk), NetWare and Windows for Workgroups. It comes with four or eight ports, each capable of up to 64Kb/s data rates. Therefore, it can be connected to high-speed modems or even ISDN links.
(800) 458-3550 or (617) 270-8300

UDS Motorola
LanFast
Available in versions for Ethernet or token ring, LanFast is a high-speed data V.32bis modem that connects directly to a network. It offers single-session remote access with the highest possible performance. A unique feature is Charge Back, which prompts remote users for a phone number, then calls them back at their home or hotel. (Other products of this type have call-back security, but only to one predefined site.) The LanFast is also sold as the LanModem by Microtest.
(800) 451-2369 or (205) 430-8000

US Robotics
Shared Access Server
USR's shared access server incorporates a built-in high-speed modem and a 386SX host PC. Therefore, it offers both remote access and the option of remote control (screen sharing).
(800) 342-5877 or (708) 982-5010

Routers

3Com
NetBuilder II
3Com's NetBuilder II comes in two models, with four or eight communications slots. It has a so-called Communications Engine Card with an AMD 29000 RISC processor and 12MB of RAM. Interface cards, available separately, include Ethernet, token ring, WAN and FDDI. You can add and remove cards without even powering down the router. SNA and SDLC support is planned, while support for SNMP management is extensive.
(800) NET-3COM (638-3266)

Cisco
AGS+/4
The standard by which many routers have been measured, Cisco's AGS+/4 contains a Motorola 68040 engine and several processors linked by a high-speed data bus. It supports more than 20 network protocols and every available hardware architecture except ARCnet. Manageable via SNMP, Telnet or TFTP, it also connects well to an IBM SNA/SDLC environment.
(800) 553-6387 or (415) 326-1941

Hewlett-Packard
Router ER
HP's Router ER is not as flexible as some others, but rewards the user with simplicity—it lacks even a power switch. Once a terminal is connected, you'll see an easy-to-use configuration menu with context-sensitive help. It routes IPX, IP, AppleTalk and DECnet Phase IV. The Router ER also has extensive filtering capabilities, letting a network manager forward data selectively.
(800) 752-0900 or Fast Fax info (800) 333-1917

IBM

6611 Network Processor

A desktop-style box with a Micro Channel bus, the 6611 resembles a PC. Like a PC, it may be configured by Windows or X-Windows software. However, it features up to seven interface cards (Ethernet, token ring, TI serial, X.25, SDLC), each with its own RISC processor. Therefore, it can merge IBM mainframe SNA traffic onto a multiprotocol wide area network.

(800) 772-2227

Novell

MultiProtocol Router, Version 2.0

NetWare 3.11 and 4.0 already have some routing capabilities, invoked when you install multiple interface cards in a single server. MultiProtocol Router software adds OSI and SNMP support plus better filtering. Of course, it's tuned toward routing the IPX protocol native to NetWare.

(800) 638-9273

Proteon

CNX-500

The three-slot CNX-500 uses an AMD 29000 RISC processor. It routes IP, IPX, DECNet Phase IV and DECNet OSI via both Ethernet and token ring.

(800) 545-7464 or (508) 898-2800

Proteon

ProNet DNX-300m

Relatively low-priced, the DNX-300m supports VINES and SNA as well as IP, IPX and AppleTalk. Unlike some other units, it will bridge all traffic that can't be routed. With a 386 processor and

2.5MB of RAM, it has room for one communications card only, but this can support up to four ports.
(800) 545-7464 or (508) 898-2800

Tribe
TribeStar
The TribeStar is a hub with eight LocalTalk ports and one Ethernet port. By giving each LocalTalk port its own channel to Ethernet, it claims to deliver about 50 to 80 percent of the speed increase you'd get from a complete Ethernet upgrade.
(510) 814-3900

Servers

Advanced Logic Research
ProVEISA SMP 4/66d
The SMP 4/66d is a massive unit that accepts 12 drive bays, 12 EISA slots and one or two processors. As a multiprocessor server, it can run SCO Unix, Novell's SFT III, Banyan's VINES SMP and Microsoft's Windows NT.
(800) 444-4257

Advanced Logic Research
ProVEISA VM 4/66d
ALR's ProVEISA is an economy-priced tower using a 66MHz 486 processor. It features room for 12 drives (five externally accessible), two cooling fans and a 300-watt power supply. There are six EISA expansion slots and two ISA slots. The motherboard can handle up to 256MB of RAM on board and features an upgradable processor.
(800) 444-4257

Advanced Logic Research

Evolution V Pentium

This massive machine includes a 60MHz or 66MHz Pentium processor, true 64-bit memory architecture (expandable to 1GB of RAM) and three VESA-standard local bus slots. Also included are 13 drive bays and a 415-watt power supply.

(800) 444-4257

Apple

Workgroup Server 95

Based on the Macintosh Quadra 950, the Server 95 runs Apple's new AppleShare Pro file and print server software (which is Unix-based). It also includes a local-bus card featuring 128K of static RAM cache and two SCSI DMA channels. The latter exploit A/UX's asynchronous I/O capabilities. In addition to a 33MHz 68040 processor, the Server 95 features four storage bays, five Nu-Bus slots and an integrated Ethernet connector.

(800) 776-2333 or (408) 996-1010

AST

Premium SE 4/66d

The Premium SE's large tower case has a 300-watt power supply, extensive bracing and even padding to help keep expansion boards firmly seated. It offers ten EISA slots, a removable processor board and eleven drive bays. Also included is a FastSCSI disk controller that configures drive arrays for RAID Levels 0, 1, 5 or 6.

(800) 876-4278

AST

Manhattan SMP

This high-end server product features error-corrected memory and optional dual power supplies. It offers nine EISA expansion slots

and 16 drive bays. Featuring fully symmetric multiprocessing, it has up to six 486 CPU cards and provisions for Pentium.
(800) 876-4278

Compaq
ProSignia 486DX2/66
Compaq's ProSignia tower has eight drive bays and seven EISA slots. Its power supply is 240 watts and RAM is expandable to 128MB. Unusual features include an internal Fast SCSI-2 connector and *Insight* server-management software. The latter enables temperature sensing, remote notification, drive controller duplexing and automatic server recovery.
(800) 345-1518 or (713) 370-0670

Compaq
SystemPro/XL
Compaq's third-generation file server, the SystemPro/XL features dual-processor support and error-correcting (ECC) RAM chips. A new recovery feature lets the system restart itself after a crash, simultaneously dialing a system administrator's beeper. The SystemPro/XL also records system errors in an area of nonvolatile RAM.
(800) 345-1518

Hewlett-Packard
NetServer LE
HP's NetServer LE comes with five open EISA expansion slots, four mass-storage shelves and many integrated features. Unlike previous-generation servers, it offers onboard Super VGA, IDE and Fast SCSI-2 controllers. The CPU can be either a 33MHz 486SX, 33MHz 486DX or 33/66MHz 486DX2.
(800) 752-0900

Hewlett-Packard

NetServer LM

Hewlett-Packard's massive NetServer LM holds nine drives—all accessible externally—and a 396-watt power supply. It has eight EISA expansion slots and a Pentium-based processor module. With an internal SCSI adapter, it supports an optional 8GB drive array. Maximum RAM is 348MB.
(800) 752-0900

IBM

PS/2 Server 195

IBM's PS/2 Server 195 comes with eight Micro Channel expansion slots, a 486/50 processor and RISC coprocessors on each of its SCSI channels plus its memory controller. With the Maximum Availability and Support System/2 (MASS/2) option, it provides comprehensive local and remote server monitoring, control, turning and recovery. Also available is a RAID Level 5 disk array.
(800) 772-2227

IBM

PS/2 Server 295

The PS/2 Server 295 comes with 12 Micro Channel slots, single or dual 486 processors and MASS/2 monitoring.
(800) 772-2227

NEC

Express/II P66LT and Express/II P662LT

NEC's new high-end servers feature up to 386MB of RAM, an integrated dual-channel SCSI-2 interface and a 66MB/s implementation of the EISA bus. The Express/II P662LT's dual-processing design accepts ECC memory and up to two Pentium processors.
(800) 632-4636

NEC

PowerMate Express 486DX2/66te

NEC's PowerMate Express 486DX2/66 comes in a large case with a 368-watt power supply, three fans and room for 11 drives. There are ten EISA expansion slots, and RAM is expandable to 256MB. (800) 632-4636

Zenith

ZDS Z-Server 450DE

The Z-Server's case has a 384-watt power supply, eight EISA expansion slots and room for 11 disk drives. Upgradable to the Pentium processor, the Z-Server also accepts an unusually hefty 384MB of RAM.

(800) 553-0331 or (708) 808-5000

PART THREE

Bibliography

Books

Borland, R., L.L. Lorenz, & R.M. O'Mara. *Windows for Workgroups Companion*, Microsoft Press, 1993.

CAL Industries Staff. *Local Area Networks: Developing Your System for Business*. John Wiley & Sons, 1989.
Analyzes various LAN options from a business perspective. Offers valuable advice for forming and running network steering committees. Emphasizes LAN selection and installation.

Corrigan, Patrick, and Aisling Guy. *Building Local Area Networks with Novell's NetWare*. M&T Books, 1989.
A good basic reference book for *NetWare* administrators. Contains a useful appendix for using Macintosh computers with *NetWare*.

Durr, Michael, and Mark Gibbs. *Networking Personal Computers*, 3d Ed. Que Corporation, 1989.
A thorough and complete overview of networking technology and management issues, especially strong in addressing security issues. Not specific to any network operating system.

Feldman, P. & T. Rugg. *NetWare Lite Made Easy*, Osborne/McGraw-Hill, 1993.

Hader, Michael L. *Mastering NetWare*. Hayden Books, 1989.

Kosiur, David R. & Nancy E.H. Jones. *Macworld Networking Handbook*, IDG Books, 1992.

McCann, John T. *NetWare Supervisor's Guide*. M&T Books, 1990.
An excellent technical reference for Novell's *NetWare* operating system. Contains a wealth of otherwise hard-to-find technical details and bug documentation. Includes far more information about managing and troubleshooting an existing network than most other books. One of the most popular books among Novell LAN administrators.

Needleman, Rafael. *InfoWorld: Understanding Networks*. InfoWorld Publishing Corp., 1990.

O'Dell, Peter. *The Computer Networking Book*, Ventana Press, 1989.
A good introduction to networking options for an organization considering a LAN. Uses non-technical business arguments to evaluate various alternatives and even suggests short-term alternatives.

Rinzler, Alan and David Gancher, eds. *The ComputerLand Guide to Local Area Networks.* ComputerLand Books, 1990.
Offers a clear and comprehensive introduction to LAN technology and maintenance issues. Includes a buyer's guide listing important LAN products.

Veljkov, Mark. *MacLans: Local Area Networking with the Macintosh.* Scott, Foresman & Co., 1989.
Explores networking Macintosh computers with PCs.

Magazines

We strongly recommend all of the dedicated LAN magazines. They each provide detailed information about the latest in LAN technology and management issues. Many of the more general computing magazines also offer excellent articles about LANs and LAN issues.

LAN Magazine. Miller Freeman Publications, 600 Harrison St., San Francisco, CA 94107. (415) 905-2234

LAN Times. McGraw-Hill, 7050 Union Park Center, Suite 240, Midvale, UT 80407.

Network Computing. CMP Publications, Inc., 600 Community Drive, Manhasset, NY 11030. (516) 562-5071

PC Week. 800 Boylston St., Boston, MA 02199. (615) 375-4000
This weekly publication keeps up with fast-breaking news in the computer industry. A special section called "Connectivity" deals primarily with networking.

Other Publications

Netware Advisor. Bicamiss Systems Group, P.O. Box 27966, Houston, TX 77227.

NetWare Technical Journal, Novell Corp., Provo, UT 84606. (800) 453-1267

Glossary

access method
The component of the data link (layer 2 of the OSI Model) functions that determines which node is next to use the LAN; a set of rules used to direct traffic on the network. The access method—how a LAN governs users' electrical access to the cable—significantly affects the LAN's features and performance. Examples of access methods are token passing, used by ARCnet and token ring, and Carrier Sense Multiple Access with Collision Detection, used by Ethernet. (See CSMA/CD.)

address
A set of numbers that uniquely identifies something: a workstation on a LAN, a location in computer memory, the next hop in a route.

Address Resolution Protocol (ARP)
Protocol used by TCP/IP to associate IP addresses with MAC-layer addresses, such as Ethernet addresses.

algorithm
A "recipe" for making a computer do something; a sequence of steps followed by a computer to accomplish a task.

ANSI

American National Standards Institute, an organization that helps set voluntary standards and also represents the United States in some international standards bodies.

AppleTalk

A software standard from Apple Computer Corporation that facilitates linking Macintosh computers and peripherals. AppleTalk may now be run over Ethernet and token ring networks—using NetWare servers and other non-Macintosh systems—at a variety of speeds. Should not be confused with LocalTalk, the 230Mbits/sec networking hardware that is built into every Macintosh computer.

AppleTalk File Protocol

The application-layer (layer 7 of the OSI Model) protocol used to provide file services to Macintosh clients.

application

A software program that carries out some useful task. Database managers, spreadsheets, communications packages, graphics programs and word processors are all applications. Application software should be distinguished from system software, the software used by the computer itself to accomplish tasks for application software. Network operating systems are also considered part of system software. DOS, OS/2, NetWare, MVS, 3+ and Unix are all examples of system software.

application layer

Layer 7 of the OSI Model. Application software, which in this context includes network and workstation operating system software, employs application-layer protocols to request and provide services over the network. Application-layer functions include file handling, message handling, directory services, network management and many others.

application program interface (API)

A set of commands and data formats, typically tied to a programming language, for programmers to use in developing applications. APIs simplify program development or furnish special functions, such as graphical user interface components. An API can make it simple for developers to implement a protocol.

architecture

The way hardware or software is structured: how the system or program is constructed, how its components fit together, and the protocols and interfaces used for communication and cooperation among modules or components of the system. Network architecture defines the functions and descriptions of data formats and procedures used for communication between nodes or workstations.

ARCnet

Attached Resource Computer Network. A 2.5Mbits/sec LAN that uses a modified token-passing protocol. The advantages of ARCnet are ease of installation and use, well-documented technology, a star-wired topology and the use of coaxial cable. Some ARCnet vendors support twisted-pair cable.

ASCII

American Standard Code for Information Interchange. A standard set of characters—alphabetical, numerical and symbolic ($, @, % and so on)—recognized by most computer systems. A presentation-layer (layer 6 of the OSI Model) protocol.

asynchronous

A type of data transmission that does not require equal time intervals between units of data. (See synchronous.)

ATM

Asynchronous Transfer Mode, a connection-oriented wide area and local area technology based on high-speed switching of 53-byte cells. Capable of transmitting high-bandwidth data, such as high-resolution video, in realtime.

audit trail

A record of events. Network operating systems can be set up to keep a record of who uses what resources at what time—an important tool for network management, especially accounting and security management.

back end

The part of a database server that performs data storage, retrieval, management and security functions. Complementary to the front end, which interfaces with the user and formats data for presentation. The back end is often called the server. The front end is often called the client. (See client-server model.)

backup

To copy in case the original is destroyed. "Backup" can be a verb, as in, "I backup the hard disk so I don't lose anything." It can be an adjective, as in, "I just bought a backup disk," or a noun, as in, "Tape backup is very important on a LAN." A backup copy of a file is a second copy, stored on tape, floppy disk or hard disk. Backup ensures that if the original copy is destroyed or damaged, the file can be restored, at least partially.

bandwidth

The capacity of a device or connection to carry information usually measured in bits per second (bps). In a network, the greater the bandwidth, the greater the information-carrying capacity of the network, and the faster the data can be transmitted from one device to another.

baseband

One of two types of LAN connections. In baseband LANs, the entire bandwidth of the cable is used to transmit a single digital signal. In the electronically more sophisticated broadband LAN, the bandwidth is divided into many channels, so it can simultaneously transmit video, voice and data. Baseband digital signals are put directly onto the cable without modulation. Multiple concurrent transmissions are achieved by time division multiplexing. (See broadband, multiplexing.)

batch processing

A type of data processing whereby related transactions are grouped, transmitted and processed together by the same computer at the same time. In batch processing, immediate responses are not needed, and no user input is required while the processing takes place. An example of batch processing is corporate payroll. All the employees' weekly times are processed at one time. The complementary class of data processing is realtime. (See realtime.) A network can handle both classes of data processing.

Bindery

The database on a Novell NetWare server that keeps track of users, groups, access privileges, passwords and other internal objects. Access to the Bindery is crucial for configuration management and administration on NetWare networks.

block
A collection of transmitted information that is seen as a discrete entity. Usually has its own address, control, routing and error checking information. (See also packet and packet switching.)

bridge
A device that can connect two or more networks, provided that they employ the same data link protocols.

broadband
One of two types of LAN connections. In broadband networks, the cable can carry video, voice and data traffic simultaneously. Signals on a cable are multiplexed by frequency division rather than by time division. Because all nodes require special modems and cable requirements are more exacting, broadband networks are more costly and complex than baseband. (See baseband.)

broadcast message
A message from one user sent to all nodes on a segment or all nodes of a certain class.

brouter
A networking device that combines some of the capabilities of a bridge with those of a router; that is, it can perform routing for some network-layer protocols but acts as a bridge when it encounters other protocols. (See bridge, router.)

buffer
Storage space in RAM (or a separate device) used to compensate for differences between the speed of data transmission and the speed with which the data can be serviced by temporarily holding the transmission.

bulletin board system (BBS)
An electronic message system with centralized mailboxes and posting areas. Users can dial in, leave messages and read messages. Sometimes confused with an electronic mail system (which has distributed mailboxes).

bus topology
A one-cable LAN, in which all workstations are connected to a single cable. On a bus network, all workstations hear all transmissions on the cable simultaneously. Each workstation then selects those transmissions addressed to it based on address information contained in the transmission. It is possible to connect bus networks together, using a bridge.

byte

A group of 8 bits, often used to represent a character. Bytes are also units of storage and transmission. The SNMP standards refer to "octets" instead of bytes, apparently because in some terminologies bytes can have more or fewer than 8 bits.

cache

An area of high-speed RAM specifically set aside to improve system performance. Blocks of data are automatically copied from a system's disk drive or main memory area into the cache, which is then used to execute instructions as quickly as possible.

CAD

Computer-Aided Design.

CCITT

Comité Consultatif Internationale Télégraphique et Téléphonique, a committee of the International Telecommunications Union, which is one of the agencies of the United Nations. The members of CCITT are the world's telephone and telegraph government agencies. CCITT standards include the V.32 modem transmission, V.42 error correction and X.25 packet switching standards.

client-server model

An architecture for applications programs under which the software is split into two parts: client and server. The server component provides services for the client part, which interacts with the user. The two parts can run on different machines. The most common client-server application is the database server. This is a database management system (DBMS) where the functions are split into a "front end" (client) that interacts with the user to enter data, issue queries and produce reports, and a "back end" (server) that stores the data, controls access, responds to queries, protects the data and makes necessary changes. The main advantages of the client-server model are reduced network traffic, much improved performance, greater flexibility in application development and improved availability of data.

CMIP (Common Management Information Protocol)

The OSI network management standard, much less commonly implemented today than SNMP.

CMOT (CMIP Over TCP/IP)
A now-defunct scheme for transporting CMIP management information over TCP/IP protocols.

coaxial cable
An electrical cable in which a solid piece of metal wire is surrounded by insulation and then surrounded by shielding whose center coincides with the center of the piece of wire—hence the term coaxial. Coaxial cables have wide bandwidth and can carry many data, voice and video conversations simultaneously. Cable TV runs on coaxial cable.

collision
The result of two nodes trying to use a shared transmission medium simultaneously. The electrical signals interfere with each other, which ruins both messages and forces the nodes to retransmit.

collision detection
The process of detecting simultaneous (and therefore mutually interfering) transmission. (See CSMA/CD.)

communications server
A type of gateway that translates the packetized information on a LAN into the formats used on telephone lines or on direct connections to minicomputers and mainframes. It allows nodes on a LAN to share modems or host connections.

concentrator
A central cabling source for physical-star wired networks. Performs the same functions as a hub, but may be larger and more modular.

configuration
The set of all variables that can be changed or adjusted for hardware devices or software routines. Configurations may be effected via switch settings, jumpers, software instructions, setup programs and the like.

configuration management
Identifying the components of the network, verifying that they have been set up correctly, tracking them as they attach and detach and changing their installation parameters as the network grows and changes or as problems are identified.

CRC

Cyclic Redundancy Check, an error detection technique that works by calculating a checksum for a piece of digital information that is appended to the information. The destination node recalculates the checksum and compares it to the appended checksum. If they don't match, it declares the existence of an error.

crosstalk

The introduction of signals from one communication channel into another.

CSMA/CD

Carrier Sense Multiple Access With Collision Detection. When access to the network is needed, this system verifies that the network is free. If it isn't, it waits a certain amount of time before checking again. If the network is free, yet two or more devices try to gain access at the very same time, it forces them to back off so that they don't collide, and then tries again.

database server

The back-end part of a client-server database. (See client-server model.) It controls the data, granting access to multiple users, updating and deleting records, performing queries and generating reports.

DBMS

Database Management System, a program or collection of programs that creates and maintains a database and allows users to retrieve information from it.

destination address

That part of a message that indicates for whom the message is intended.

diskless PC

A PC without a disk drive. Used on a LAN, a diskless PC runs by booting DOS or another operating system from the file server. It does this via a read-only memory chip on its network interface card called a remote boot ROM. When the machine is turned on, programs in this boot ROM are executed. They go out over the network to the file server and look for the operating system to be loaded into the diskless PC's memory. The file server acts as the disk for the diskless PC. Sometimes cheaper than PCs with disks, diskless PCs can also be more compact and offer better security.

distributed database

A database that has components in more than one place. Controlling access and synchronizing updates on distributed databases are very difficult problems.

distributed data processing

The processing of information in separate locations equipped with independent computers. The computers are connected by a network, even though the processing is geographically dispersed. Often a more efficient use of computer processing power because each CPU can be devoted to a certain task.

DMA

Direct Memory Access. By using a DMA channel, data can rapidly move between a computer's main memory and a peripheral, such as a LAN interface card.

DOS

Disk Operating System, a program or set of programs that instruct a disk-based computing system to schedule and supervise tasks, manage computer resources and operate and control peripheral devices, including disk drives, keyboards, screens and printers. Often used as shorthand for Microsoft's MS-DOS or IBM's PC DOS, the most commonly encountered disk operating systems on Intel chip-based computers. (See also NOS.)

downsize

To move a business application from one computing platform to a smaller, less expensive type of computer. Many applications were first downsized from mainframes to minicomputers, and are now moving from minis to microcomputer-based networks.

driver

A software program, designed as an extension to an operating system, that contains the information necessary to work with other devices or protocols.

duplex

Refers to whether a communications link can transmit and receive simultaneously or perform only one of the two functions at a time. A full-duplex link does both, while a half-duplex link can—like a two-way radio—do only one at a time.

duplexing

Providing two identical disk drives and controllers so that one of them can take over in case the other fails. Mirroring is similar but involves less hardware duplication. It uses a single disk controller to save data to two different disk drives.

EIA

Electronics Industries Association, a U.S. trade organization that issues its own standards and contributes to ANSI.

802.3

The numerical designation for the IEEE (Institute of Electrical and Electronic Engineers) standard governing the use of the CSMA/CD media-access method.

electronic mail

A messaging system operating over some sort of communications medium, often a LAN.

e-mail

Electronic mail.

Ethernet

A CSMA/CD, 10Mbits/sec network developed at Xerox's Palo Alto Research Center, one of the most popular baseband LANs in use. DEC and Intel participated with Xerox to make Ethernet a network standard that provides computers with network access on a transmit-at-will basis. If two transmissions collide, the nodes wait a random interval and try again until they get through. Ethernet runs on coaxial cable, fiber-optic cable or twisted-pair wiring.

fiber-optic cable

A data transmission medium consisting of glass fibers. Light-emitting diodes send light through the fiber to a detector, which converts the light back into electrical signals. Fiber-optic cable may be the predominant medium for LANs in the future. Fiber-optic cable offers immense bandwidth plus protection from eavesdropping, electromagnetic interference and radioactivity.

file locking

A method of ensuring data integrity. With a file-locking system, only one user can update a file at a time. Other users are locked out, unable to access the file. (See also record locking.)

file server

Any device that provides file storage and retrieval services over a LAN, typically a computer with high I/O and disk drive performance and high data storage capacity.

frame relay

A wide area technology that offers higher performance than X.25 packet switching by eliminating much of the error-checking and packet-sequencing overhead of the older technology. It allows a customer's available bandwidth to jump momentarily as much as 50 percent, which provides a good match for the "bursty" nature of network traffic.

front end

The component of a client-server system concerned with formatting and presenting data to a user. Also called the client.

gateway

A device that can connect two or more dissimilar networks, or connect a network to a mainframe or minicomputer. A gateway can convert all seven layers of the OSI Model. (See OSI Model.) In Internet terminology, a gateway is a node that can forward packets to other nodes—what would be called a router anywhere else.

groupware

Also called collaborative computing or workgroup computing. Groupware includes programs designed to handle group-related tasks such as scheduling meetings, sending messages and other information, and coauthoring documents. Other groupware includes networked bulletin board systems and group decision support systems.

handshake

A preliminary procedure, usually part of a communications protocol, to establish a connection. Sometimes, during the handshake, two computers exchange the conditions under which they will communicate. Other times, they just alert each other to the impending communication.

header

The beginning part of a message, which contains destination address, source address and other information.

host

Traditionally, a computer system, usually a mainframe or minicomputer, that provides computer service for a number of users. In Internet terminology, nodes are either hosts or gateways. Hosts are incapable of forwarding packets.

hub

The device that functions as the physical and electrical center of a star topology network or cabling system. Connections to all the nodes radiate from the hub.

interface

A demarcation between two devices, where the electrical signals, connectors, timing and handshaking meet. Often the procedures, codes and protocols that enable the two devices to interact are included or carried out by the interface. An example is an RS-232-C port. Some of its 25 pins are used to send information and make sure devices can talk to each other. The pins carry different messages, such as "request to send," "acknowledgment" and others.

interface card

A printed circuit board fitting in the expansion chassis of a computer to make the physical connection between computer and LAN cable. The interface card is responsible for getting raw bits from the computer onto the network and vice versa. This requires translation from parallel to serial form and back, buffering, packet creation, encoding/decoding, cable access, and transmission and reception.

IP

Internet Protocol. (See TCP/IP.)

ISO

The International Standards Organization (ISO) is an umbrella group of standards organizations (including the American National Standards Institute or ANSI) from some 90 countries. These nongovernmental organizations define standard industrial and commercial practices for many classes of products. The Open Standards Interconnect (OSI) committee of the ISO is responsible for electronic network standards, including the 7-layer OSI Reference Model.

K

A standard quantity measurement of computer storage. One K is loosely defined as 1,000 bytes; in fact it is 1,024 bytes, which is the equivalent of 2 to the tenth power.

LAN

Local area network.

LAN adapter

Hardware designed to permit a personal computer to attach to a LAN. Usually supplied on a removable circuit board known as a network interface card (NIC), but may also be built onto a PC's motherboard or designed as an external unit.

LAN Manager

A network operating system from Microsoft for servers running OS/2.

LAN Server

IBM's network operating system based on OS/2. It provides the traditional services of a network operating system for workstations that can run either DOS or OS/2. It runs under OS/2 on a server PC and provides file and print sharing, communications, messaging and other services.

local area network

A data communications network, also known as a LAN, spanning a limited geographical area—a few miles at most. It provides communication between computers and peripherals.

logical drive

Disk storage on a network server, represented logically by a name or letter to facilitate access from user workstations. For example, the storage available on a NetWare server might appear to users as if it were a drive E on their PCs.

log-in

The process of identifying and authenticating oneself to a computer system. Used to control access to computer systems or networks.

MAC

Medium Access Control, one of the two sublayers of the data link layer.

mainframe

A large computer usually supplied with peripherals and software by a single large vendor, often with a closed architecture. Mainframes almost always use dumb terminals, connected in star configurations.

Mbits/sec

Megabits per second, or million bits per second.

minicomputer

A small or medium-sized computer accessed by dumb terminals. A minicomputer is bigger and may be more powerful than a PC.

mirroring

Writing identical information to two separate disk drives so that one of them can take over from the other in the event of hardware failure. Duplexing is similar, but involves more hardware duplication. (See duplexing.)

modem

A device (modulator/demodulator) that converts digital data from a transmitting device into a signal suitable for transmission over a telephone (analog) channel. At the other end, another modem reconverts the analog signal to digital data for use by the computer.

MS-DOS

Microsoft Disk Operating System, the standard operating system for computers equipped with the Intel 8086, 8088 and 80286 (and subsequent) microprocessors. PC-DOS is IBM's version of MS-DOS.

multiplexing

The transmission of multiple signals over a single communications line. Frequency domain multiplexing modulates signals onto different carrier frequencies (like the multiple signals carried over TV cables). Time domain multiplexing separates signals by sending one after the other.

multiprocessing

Running the same application on multiple processors concurrently. Symmetrical multiprocessing processors act sequentially on the next instruction when they have finished an operation. Asymmetrical multiprocessing processors have particular assigned tasks; if these tasks don't need doing, they wait idly.

multitasking

The concurrent operation of two or more programs by a single computer.

multithreading

Like multitasking, the concurrent operation of two or more tasks by a single computer. The difference here is that the tasks may be components, or "threads," of a single application rather than being separate programs.

multiuser
Having the ability to support multiple users with a single computer while providing a full range of capability to each one.

NetBIOS
Network Basic Input/Output System. Part of the original IBM PC network program. Like the BIOS of an individual computer, NetBIOS is an interface that applications use to gain access to computer resources on a network instead of in just one machine.

NetWare
The most popular network operating system, produced by Novell, and supported by almost every hardware and software manufacturer. Available in a variety of versions, including NetWare 3.11, which uses special functions of the 80386 processor for more rapid operation; NetWare 4.0, which includes enterprise-wide directory services; NetWare 2.2, which can run on computers with 80286 processors; and NetWare Lite, which offers inexpensive peer-to-peer networking services to small workgroups. NetWare for the Macintosh allows DOS PCs and Macintosh computers to be interconnected. NetWare 3.11 and above also supports OS/2 and Unix workstations.

network architecture
The structures and protocols of a computer network. (See architecture.)

network interface controller
Electronic circuitry that connects a node to a network. Usually a card that fits into one of the expansion slots inside a personal computer.

network topology
The geography of a network: whether it is a star, a bus or a ring. The physical, electrical and logical topologies of a network can be different. Token ring networks are typically physical stars but logical and electrical rings. A 10BASE-T Ethernet network is usually a physical and logical star but an electrical bus.

node
A point in a network where service is provided, service is used or communications channels are interconnected.

noise

Random electrical signals, generated by circuit components or by natural disturbances, that introduce errors into transmitted data. Noise can come from lightning, nearby cables, electrical motors, radio transmissions, sunspots and other sources.

NOS

Network Operating System, a program or set of programs that instructs a computer to provide services (especially file, print and communications services) for clients on a network. Examples of NOS software include NetWare, *LAN Manager* and the *AppleShare File Server*. NOS server software cooperates with client software components that request services. These software components, often known as redirectors or network shells, make a workstation and its disk operating system (see DOS) aware of the server and able to access it. Apple's System 7 software is a disk operating system that can also act as a NOS for small workgroups.

object

A unit of an object-oriented program, consisting of both data and rules for behavior. SNMP and CMIP define a large number of managed objects that provide developers with a framework for writing management applications software. Also, any item with an entry in the NetWare Bindery database, including users, groups, access privileges and passwords. This usage is unrelated to object-oriented programming.

online

The state of a peripheral, such as a printer, modem, terminal or LAN workstation, when it is connected and ready to operate.

Oracle

A relational database management program from Oracle Corporation. Popular as a back end for client-server databases. It supports SQL and runs on personal computers, minis and mainframes. (See client-server model.)

OSI Model

Open System Interconnection Model, a paradigm established by the International Standards Organization (ISO) for communications worldwide. It divides all networking services among seven layers: physical, data link, network, transport, session, presentation and application.

OS/2

An operating system codeveloped by Microsoft and IBM to exploit the power and speed of personal computers based on the Intel 80286, 80386 and 80486 microprocessors. Key features include support of multitasking and programs larger than 640K, sophisticated memory management capabilities, a graphical user interface and process-to-process communications facilities. OS/2's multitasking can form the basis for distributed applications on LANs.

OS/2 Extended Edition

IBM's proprietary extension to OS/2, which, among other things, allows a workstation to work in conjunction with IBM minicomputers and mainframes. Also includes a database management system.

packet

A sequence of bits, including a header, consisting of addresses, control elements and data. It constitutes a unit for the operations of a particular layer of the OSI Model. Packets are often associated with layer 3, the network layer. At the data link layer, the layer 3 packet has a header and a trailer and is often referred to as a frame.

packet buffer

Memory space set aside for storing a packet awaiting transmission or for storing a received packet. The memory may be located in the network interface controller or in the computer to which the controller is connected. (See buffer.)

packet switching

A data transmission method, using packets, whereby a channel is occupied only for the duration of transmission of the packet. The packet switch sends the different packets from different data conversations along the best route available in any order. At the other end, the packets are reassembled to form the original message, which is then sent to the receiving computer. Because packets need not be sent in a particular order, and because they can go any route as long as they reach their destination, packet-switching networks can choose the most efficient route and send the most efficient number of packets down that route before switching to another route to send more packets.

PC

Personal computer.

peer-to-peer

A description of communications between two equal devices, in contrast to terminal-host communications. Under the latter, a mainframe does all the processing, and the communicating devices, including PCs, act like terminals, just doing input and output. With peer-to-peer communications, both computers execute applications, which can request services from each other and reply to requests.

peripheral

Any hardware device connected to a computer that is not itself a computer. Examples include modems, monitors, printers, disk drives, scanners and mice.

platform

(1) A family of computers, such as the Intel platform or the Macintosh platform. (2) A software foundation for other programs, such as the Windows platform. Novell's *NetWare Management System*, Hewlett-Packard's *OpenView* and Sun's *SunNet Manager* are all software platforms for network management application software, providing basic application services for other developers. (3) A standard configuration of, for instance, a workstation, a server or a network printer. These configuration platforms provide a base system that is known to work properly; modifications to the platform can be backed out when there is any suspicion that they may be the cause of a problem.

print server

A process that runs on a file server or a workstation and provides print queues and printing services to applications on the network.

protocols

The rules that govern the format, timing, sequencing and error-control mechanisms for data moving through a network. By establishing where to look in a stream of bits to find data relevant to a particular service, protocols make network traffic intelligible. Protocols from particular vendors or other common sources often form families of protocols. These families of protocols are often referred to as suites of protocols or protocol stacks. IPX is a network-layer protocol (see OSI Model) employed by NetWare networks. EBCDIC is a presentation-layer protocol employed by IBM mainframe operating systems.

queue

A sequence or line of tasks, such as print jobs or messages, waiting for service—for processing, printing, storing, etc.

realtime

In business use, any computer system that can process multiple transactions rapidly, such as the computers for a bank's automated teller machines. More strictly, though, it refers to a computer that can respond almost instantly to signals sent to it. Examples would include an airplane autopilot or any other computer system that must monitor and control an ongoing process.

record locking

The most common and most sophisticated means for multiuser LAN applications to maintain data integrity. In a record locking system, users are prevented from working on the same data record at the same time. That way, users don't overwrite other users' changes, and data integrity is maintained. But though it doesn't allow users into the same record at the same time, record locking does allow multiple users to work on the same file simultaneously. So multiuser access is maximized. (Compare with file locking, which only allows a single user to work on a file at a time.)

repeater

A device that amplifies a signal so it can travel over a longer distance without data loss. Since it performs no other function, a repeater should not be confused with a bridge or router. (See bridge, router.)

ring

A LAN topology (organization) where each node is connected to at least two other nodes. These connections form a loop (or a ring). Data is sent from node to node around the loop in the same direction. Each node acts as a repeater by resending messages to the next node. Rings have a predictable response time, determined by the number of PCs. Network control is distributed in a ring network.

RISC

Reduced Instruction Set Computing, a microprocessor architecture designed to perform a limited number of functions, and to execute those instructions as fast as possible. Advocates of RISC processors promote their speed and low cost.

router

Routers can connect two or more networks at the network layer (layer 3 of the OSI Model) by identifying the destination network a packet is bound for and forwarding it to the next hop on the route. Because routers must unpack a packet more thoroughly than a bridge, they are often slower, more costly or both. Because they operate at the network layer, they can translate from one data link method to another (e.g., from token ring to Ethernet). Multiprotocol routers have become very desirable for the ever more common multiprotocol internetwork.

routing

The process of choosing the best path through the internetwork. Routers use various algorithms and communicate using special routing protocols to maintain routing tables. Routers look up the next hop for a packet on the table and send the packet there.

server

A computer providing a service to LAN users, such as shared access to a file system, a printer, a modem or an electronic mail system. Usually a combination of hardware and software. Servers can be PCs, minicomputers, mainframes or specialized computers designed to do nothing but dole out services to multiple users. (See file server, print server.)

shell

Novell calls its workstation client component of NetWare the shell. The shell complements DOS by redirecting service requests to the network when necessary.

SMDS

Switched Multimegabit Data Services, high-bandwidth packet switching for wide area networks, ultimately as high as 45Mbits/sec. Not currently offered by long-distance carriers, only in local telephone areas.

Sniffer

Network General Corporation's trademark for its network troubleshooting tool. A portable computer fitted with a special combination of hardware and software, the Sniffer LAN Analyzer is claimed to be the only such product that can detect problems in each of the seven layers of the OSI Model. (See OSI Model.)

SNMP

Simple Network Management Protocol, a protocol established by the Internet that allows a management station or console on a network to receive management information from and send commands to distributed management agents installed in various different entities, such as concentrators, routers or servers.

source address

The part of a message that indicates who sent the message. Often included in the header of a packet.

spooler

A program or piece of hardware that controls a buffer of data going to some output device, most commonly a printer or a tape drive. A spooler allows users to send data to a device, say a printer, even while that device is busy. The spooler controls the feeding of data to the printer by using a buffer or by creating a temporary file in which to store the data to be printed. (See buffer; compare with queue.)

SQL

Structured Query Language, a database query language invented by IBM for its mainframe databases. A version has been adopted as an ANSI standard. Most client-server database systems use SQL commands to communicate between the front end and the back end.

star topology

A topology in which each node is connected to a central hub. As an example, 10BASE-T networks use hubs or concentrators as the center of a star topology. Token ring networks that use media attachment units (MAU) consist of a physical star topology, although electrically they constitute a ring.

TCP/IP

Transmission Control Protocol/Internet Protocol, a set of communications protocols originally developed by the Department of Defense to internetwork computers. Provides file transfer and e-mail capability. Once primarily found on Unix-based and DEC VAX computers, but now supported on many other systems.

10BASE-5

The original Ethernet, a hardware implementation of the 802.3 standard (see 802.3). It is a baseband network running at 10Mbits/sec over thick coaxial cable; cable segments may be up to 500 meters in length. Also known as DIX Ethernet (for Digital, Intel and Xerox, the three vendors that worked to develop this hardware implementation). Rarely used in new network installations today because of the difficulty in handling the cable. (See 10BASE-T.)

10BASE-T

An implementation of the 802.3 standard that uses unshielded twisted-pair cabling. 10BASE-T networks run at 10Mbits/sec but cable runs are limited to 100-meter segments. Also known as twisted-pair Ethernet.

10BASE-2

Until the adoption of the 10BASE-T standard in 1990, the most common cable design for LANs. It is a baseband network running at 10Mbits/sec over thin coaxial cable; cable segments may be up to 185 meters in length. Thin coax is much cheaper and easier to handle than thick coax.

terminal emulation

The use of software on a personal computer to simulate a mainframe or mini-computer terminal. Such software is necessary because mainframes and mini-computers send terminals special characters that must be displayed as lines, boxes, alternate colors and the like. Terminals also have keys not normally found on a personal computer keyboard.

token

A unique combination of bits that circulates on a token-passing LAN. When a node receives the token, it has been given permission to transmit. (See token passing.)

token bus

A LAN with bus topology that uses token passing as its access method. ARCnet and MAP LANs are the most popular of these types of networks.

token passing

An access method. A token is passed from node to node. When a node has the token, it has permission to send a message. It then attaches the message to the token, which "carries" it around the LAN to the designated recipient. Every station in between "sees" the message, but only the receiving workstation accepts it. When the receiving station gets the message, it releases the token to be used by the next station. The entire process of generating and passing tokens around the LAN takes fractions of a second.

token ring

Type of network hardware in which individual nodes are given access to the network by a token that passes around a ring. The IEEE (Institute of Electrical and

Electronic Engineers) standard for token ring (802.5) has a raw data speed of 4Mbits/sec. Versions that work at 16Mbits/sec are also available.

topology
Description of the physical connections of a network, or the description of the possible logical connections between nodes, indicating which pairs of nodes are able to communicate. A map of the "road" between all the things attached to a LAN. Examples are bus, ring, star and tree topologies.

tree
A LAN topology in which there is only one route between any two of the nodes on the network. The pattern of connections resembles a tree.

TSR
Terminate-and-stay-resident program, a program designed to load into a computer's memory and stay there while other programs are run. In this latent state, the TSR program can be executed immediately with a special keystroke combination or transparently provide services to other programs. Often required to access a LAN. (See driver.)

twisted-pair cable
Two insulated wires wrapped around (i.e., twisted around) each other.

Unix
Computer operating system originally developed by AT&T. Also works on some personal computers. Considered to be very flexible and powerful.

virtual device
A device provided to a computer—and any applications run on that computer—via a network operating system. Virtual devices mimic actual physical devices, and include disks, serial ports and printer ports. For example, a PC connected to a LAN might seem to the user as though it has a hard disk drive, when actually that drive exists only as a virtual device—an area set aside on the hard disk of the LAN's disk server. (See logical drive.) Similarly, applications may "think" they are printing to a local printer, when actually output is being sent over the LAN to a print server. Virtual devices essentially act as a "front," hiding the LAN from users and applications software that might not otherwise be able to access it easily.

wide area network

A data communications network that includes links across a public network, such as a line leased from the local telephone company or a fiber-optic link provided by one of the long distance providers. (Private networks, where an organization may own the cable and right-of-way facilities itself, would also be considered WANs.)

Windows

Software from Microsoft. It extends the DOS operating system to include a graphical user interface. Users can view side-by-side text in multiple styles and graphics, in applications written especially for Windows (such as *Word for Windows*, *Excel* and *PageMaker*). Windows applications are increasingly being written specifically for LANs. They can, for example, display a LAN's topology on screen as a graphic, thereby simplifying the chore of LAN administration. The term "windows" may also be used generically to describe any technique through which a computer's screen is split to simultaneously display output from several programs—or components of a single program.

Windows for Workgroups

A peer-to-peer network operating system from Microsoft that runs on Intel microprocessors and support s MS Windows. Features include data sharing and printer sharing over the network, as well as background file transfers.

workstation

In the most general sense, an input/output device at which an operator works. Usually restricted to devices with their own central processing units, such as personal computers. Sometimes restricted even further, to high-resolution graphics setups with CPUs capable of running a 32bit operating system, usually Unix.

X.25

The long-time international packet switching standard. Wide area networks that cross national boundaries can usually rely on the availability of these services.

Index